PEOPLE WE KNOW, HORSES THEY LOVE

PEOPLE WE KNOW, HORSES THEY LOVE

JILL RAPPAPORT & WENDY WILKINSON

PHOTOGRAPHY BY LINDA SOLOMON

RODALE®

© 2004 by Jill Rappaport, Linda Solomon, and Wendy Wilkinson

Photographs © by Linda Solomon

Photograph on page 168 by Barry Solomon

Photographs on page 169 by Don Jones

Printed in China

Rodale Inc. makes every effort to use acid-free ♾, recycled paper ♻.

Book design by Patricia Field

LIBRARY OF CONGRESS CATALOGING-IN-PUBLICATION DATA

Rappaport, Jill.
  People we know, horses they love / Jill Rappaport and Wendy Wilkinson ; photography by Linda Solomon.
      p.   cm.
    ISBN 1-57954-857-1 hardcover
    1. Portrait photography—United States.   2. Celebrities—United States—Portraits.   3. Horsemen and horsewomen—United States—Portraits.   4. Horses—United States—Pictorial works.   I. Wilkinson, Wendy.
  II. Solomon, Linda (Linda Rappaport)   III. Title.
  TR681.F3R3617 2004
  636.1—dc22
                                                                                        2004005799

2 4 6 8 10 9 7 5 3 1   hardcover

DISTRIBUTED TO THE TRADE BY HOLTZBRINCK PUBLISHERS

RODALE
WE INSPIRE AND ENABLE PEOPLE TO IMPROVE
THEIR LIVES AND THE WORLD AROUND THEM

RODALE
LIVE YOUR WHOLE LIFE™

CONTENTS

CONTENTS

PRO AND SHOW

HEALING HANDS, HEALING HORSES

ABOUT THE AUTHORS

INTRODUCTION

In the process of creating, writing, photographing, and totally immersing ourselves in this labor of love, we discovered plenty about these people we all feel like we know. It might come as a surprise to some, but the ties that bind this remarkable group of people together have little to do with the golden privilege of celebrity and everything to do with how important, enduring, and enjoyable their relationships are with their horses. All have a deep appreciation for these marvelous creatures, along with a love for nature, freedom, and openness that is fostered in the presence of horses. As you'll come to discover yourself, some of the notables featured in the book generously contribute their time and money to take care of horses—and sometimes these strong, beautiful, and noble animals take care of them. We also noticed firsthand that how someone rides horses is frequently a reflection of how they live their life—boldly, adventurously, and with a sense of accomplishment.

Every story and image in *People We Know, Horses They Love* provides a glimpse into a very private life. We chose Robert Redford for the cover because he truly embodies the heart and soul of the book. Sundance, his magnificent ranch and refuge, began with a $500 purchase of two acres and a little cabin and has grown into a sanctuary for horses and an inspiring example of successful land preservation. Horses serve as healers and guides in the Pegasus Therapeutic Riding program, which changes lives for the better with the help of Clea Newman and the support of her parents, Paul Newman and Joanne Woodward. Clea believes that the horses and ponies that she works with and that have such a profoundly

positive effect on physically and mentally disabled people are "as close to angels as we have on earth." Our publisher agrees, and that's why Rodale is donating a portion of the book's proceeds to this worthy charity. The book also profiles Richard Gere and his wife, Carey Lowell, who are strong supporters of the Chief Joseph Foundation, which focuses on Nez Perce cultural preservation, emphasizing programs that focus on Appaloosas, Richard and Carey's beloved breed. Likewise, Hilary Duff is making a difference in the lives of wild horses as the Youth Ambassador for Return to Freedom, the American Wild Horse Sanctuary, by bringing to the forefront the plight of the American Wild Horse, which is in danger of being lost forever.

Some stories describe defining moments in a life, such as legendary Kim Novak's exclusive profile, while others offer pure enjoyment and good memories of great horse times gone by. Renowned horse gentler Buck Brannaman regards horses as equine mentors and credits them with saving him. Jack Palance, the epitome of the down-and-dirty big screen cowboy, reminisces about his role as the blacker-than-black Jack Wilson in the 1953 Western classic Shane. Now in his eighties, Jack no longer rides, but he got back in the saddle again for us. We were able to capture Hollywood leading man Dennis Quaid riding freely with his little dog Clyde across his Big Sky ranch. And we caught up with beautiful Brazilian cover girl Gisele Bundchen, who sits astride her favorite horse, Sandrino, with the passion and pure abandon that characterizes her life as one of the world's most sought-after supermodels. Kelsey and Camille Grammer, meanwhile, find joy and contentment in getting away from the rigors of Hollywood at their exquisite Malibu retreat with their beautiful steeds. And Jeff Bridges took the time to reflect on the set of *Seabiscuit* about the remarkable horse that gave hope to millions during the Depression.

We have several stories about parent and child relationships and how they have been strengthened by their shared love of horses. Alfre Woodard cherishes the bond that was formed with her twelve-year-old daughter, Mavis, through her love of horses. Chevy Chase muses over his family's almost comic interaction and just plain fun that he, his wife, Jayni, and three daughters share with their horses Bob and Candy. Katharine Ross reflects on how she rode up to her eighth month of pregnancy until she literally could not get a leg up on her horse. Daughter Cleo Elliott grew up immersed in her mother's passion for horses, which soon became her own. It

was the New York City Mounted Police that opened up the world of horses for Whoopi Goldberg and gave the young girl who lived in the projects access to these remarkable animals. Her ultimate success eventually allowed her to fulfill her dreams and finally have a farm and horses of her own.

Hope, courage, and pure inspiration are common threads that run through these intimate stories and captivating images. Renowned jockey Julie Krone keeps on racing even after suffering injuries that would sideline most riders. The core of her strength is her twenty-three-year-old Thoroughbred Peter Rabbit, who was such an important part of the family that he gave her mother the strength to battle cancer and helped Julie ultimately overcome her mother's death. Aerosmith's lead guitarist Joe Perry and his beautiful wife, Billie, adore their Friesians so much he even named his signature guitar after the breed.

Just like us, these people that we sometimes emulate and frequently admire also love these angels who have the power to heal in many special ways and give us such a sense of freedom, accomplishment, and pleasure. Those featured in *People We Know, Horses They Love* have all so graciously opened their hearts and homes to share with us, and you, a world that has so greatly enriched their lives and ours.

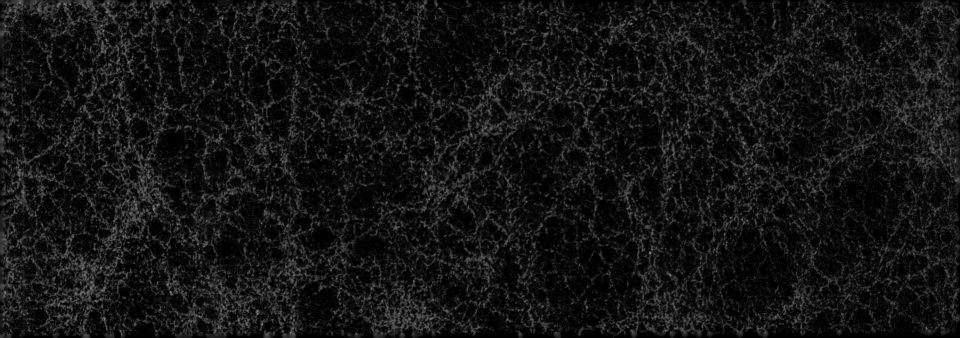

HOME ON THE RANGE

GISELE BUNDCHEN

Hailed by *Rolling Stone* magazine as the most beautiful girl in the world in 2002, Gisele Bundchen is one of the fashion industry's most sought-after and visible models. Born in Rio Grande de Sul, Brazil, Bundchen has modeled for all the top designers, including Ralph Lauren, Versace, and Valentino. With a face that has graced just about every major magazine, including *Vogue*, *Harper's Bazaar*, and *W*, she is the magnificent and multi-million-dollar beauty being featured in such advertising campaigns as Christian Dior, Dolce & Gabbana, and Missoni. In addition, Bundchen made her acting debut in the feature film *Taxi* alongside Queen Latifah and Jimmy Fallon.

A savvy businesswoman as well, Bundchen is the face of, and brains behind, Epanema, her own brand of women's foot apparel. She also serves as the spokesperson and campaign model for Fashion Target's Breast Cancer.

When not walking the runway or traveling around the world for yet another cover shoot, Bundchen can be found doing what she loves most—riding her favorite horse, Sandrino, at a private ranch in the hills of Malibu. Bundchen frequently makes the hour-and-a-half commute from her home in West Hollywood to ride her beloved European warmbloods, because only on horseback in the hills can she totally relax and experience a true sense of freedom. She also loves the discipline of hunter-jumping and frequently spends an hour in the riding ring taking Sandrino and her other horse, Aermes, through their paces.

A Sense of Freedom

Growing up in southern Brazil in a

town of less than ten thousand people, I started riding at the age of eight. I was visiting my aunt's farm during the summer, and one of the cowboys put me on a very tall gelding and hit him on the butt. Well, he took off, and I was grabbing his mane because my feet couldn't reach the stirrups. When he finally stopped—no thanks to me—instead of being scared I said, "I want to do it again!" and I have been hooked on speed ever since. Every morning that week that I was at my aunt's, I would get up early and ride all day long, galloping in one direction and then turning around and galloping back in the other direction. I fell off that horse, Carrochero, many times, but still loved it. To me it was so exciting to be on horseback. I even went on a cattle roundup and participated in several local rodeos, including riding in a team penning event. I never took a lesson in Brazil; I rode by instinct and always thought of horses as my friends.

Riding in Los Angeles has been such a different experience for me. First, I am now

riding in a tiny English saddle and there is not the big saddle horn to hold onto. Second, my horses here are so much bigger than the horses I rode in Brazil, and the style of riding is so much more disciplined. At home I would ride my horse Gallant bareback in the fields. I'd say, "Go! Go!" and just take off freely and ride as far and as long as I wanted to. But since I decided I wanted to learn how to jump, there is so much preparation involved. You have to have very strong legs for both guiding and holding on to the horse. You really have to be a good rider.

When I moved out here from New York and decided to bring horses back into my life, I had my two warmbloods, Sandrino and Aermes, shipped from Europe to the Los Angeles Equestrian Center in Burbank. It was there that I started to learn how to jump. At first I was a very green rider who probably wanted to perform beyond my ability. I fell dozens of times. I took a really bad fall on Sandrino when my feet were out of the stirrups and I was squeezing him very hard just trying to stay on. He thought I wanted to go faster, and when he approached a five-foot-tall fence I decided to jump off. I hit my head and hurt my ribs, but my trainer made me im-

mediately get into the saddle again. She said that if you can count on your two hands the number of times you've fallen off, then you are not a good rider. So I think I must be becoming a good rider—I have fallen off a lot!

Unfortunately, because of my crazy work schedule, there are some weeks when I ride every day and then I'm not on their backs for two months. I sometimes get a little jealous of my trainer because she gets to spend so much time with Sandrino and Aermes. But I don't have to ride them all the time. When I am with them, giving them carrots and lots of affection is sometimes enough for me.

Perhaps you are not supposed to say that you have a favorite horse, but I love Sandrino, my warmblood Hanoverian, so much. He is just like Speedy Gonzales. When I first saw him, I thought that he looked more like a beautiful and very elegant Thoroughbred than a thicker-built warmblood. He is so much fun. When I am at the ranch, I will take him to graze in the grassy field and then put him in the arena, where he starts running in circles. He'll look at me and start to buck and roll in the dirt. That horse seems so excited to be free, and I will clasp my hands and chase him around the arena and continue playing with him. After Sandrino is tired out, he will come up to me and I will put on his bridle, saddle him up, and start to ride. He is so sweet, and I love him to death.

Riding is such an adventure to me, especially when you and your horse are on the move and the wind is blowing through your hair. The air is fresh and the scenery is so beautiful and your mind is wandering freely, and suddenly you are hit with the realization of how wonderful life is. When I am on Sandrino, riding up into the mountains, my problems seem like a million miles away. If I am working somewhere around the world, I always have other things on my mind. I am always thinking about the next job—even when I'm sleeping, I'm thinking subliminally. The power of horses is that they make me relax and enjoy what I am doing right then and not think about what has happened in the past or what I have to do tomorrow.

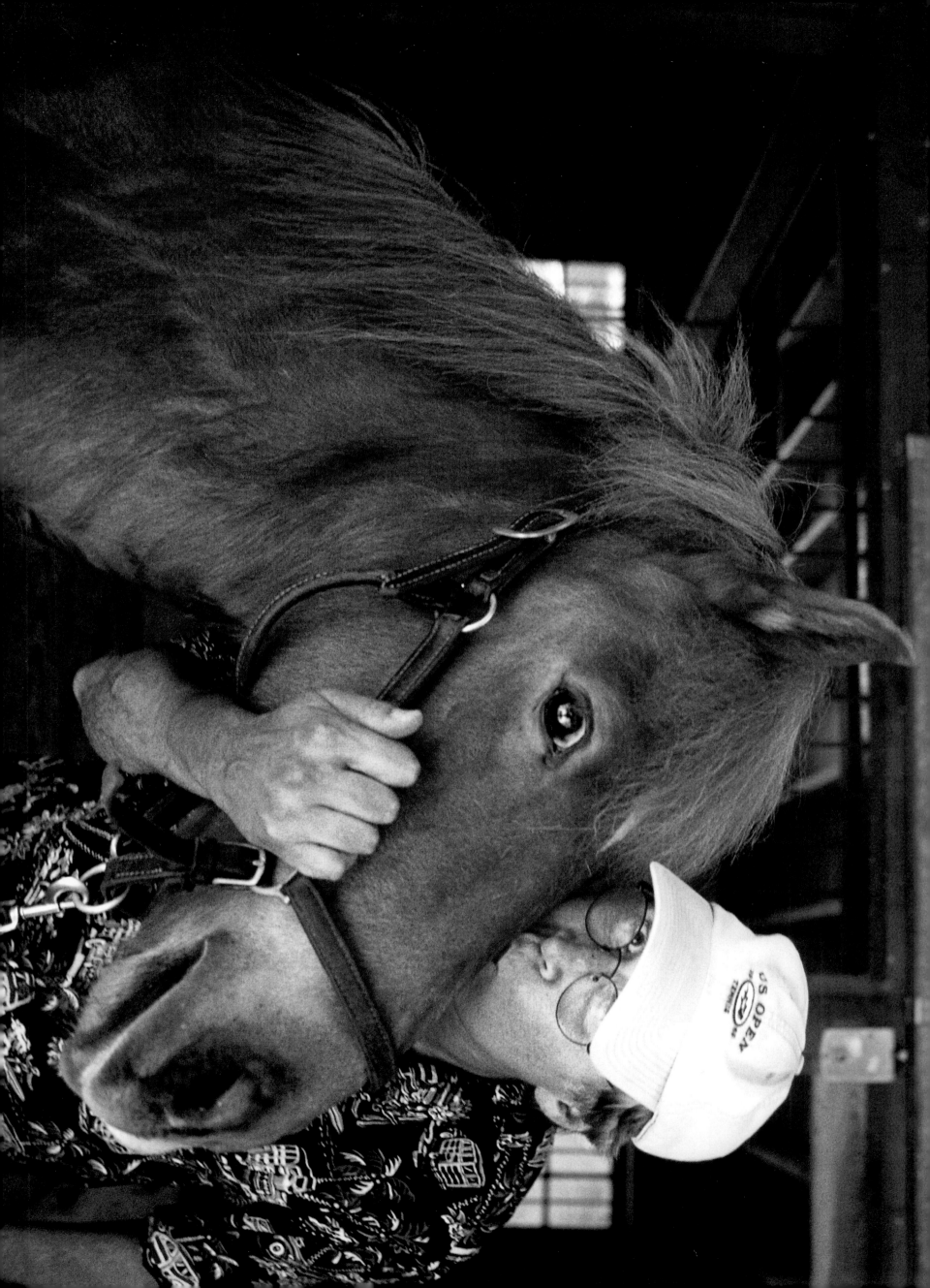

CHEVY CHASE
A (Funny) Man and His Horses

Ever since achieving nationwide popularity on the debut season of *Saturday Night Live* in 1975, Chevy Chase has been considered one of the funniest men of his generation. Initially hired on as a writer, Chase soon began appearing in front of the camera as the anchor of the popular Weekend Update segment of the show and won two Emmy Awards in the process. Chase made the transition to the big screen in *Foul Play* opposite Goldie Hawn and went on to star in *National Lampoon's Vacation*, the first of four in a series of epic misadventures of the Griswald family. Next came *Fletch, Spies Like Us, Three Amigos,* and *Fletch Lives,* in which he starred as the title character, an undercover newspaper reporter seemingly unaware of his hilarious play on words. More recently, Chase has starred in such family-oriented films as the highly successful *Snow Day* and the upcoming *Karate Dog,* and *The Great Goose Caper.*

The Chase family has found their own version of Green Acres in Bedford, New York, one of the most beautiful horse areas in the country. Along with their horses, they have chickens, tame rabbits, fish, and parrots. Chase's wife, Jayni, is quite an accomplished horsewoman, and all three daughters, Cydney, Caley, and Emily, ride as well.

"Thanks to my grandfather, Edward L. Chase, I know horses inside and out."

7

My grandfather was a great

equestrian portrait artist, so I grew up with images of horses all around me. His name was Edward L. Chase and he created *The Big Book of Horses*. The drawing in the book of a young boy jumping a horse is actually my father—my grandfather drew it from a photograph.

Although he rode, painting horses was my grandfather's passion. As a young man, he was commissioned to paint the great racehorses, including Man of War and Citation. I remember that his studio contained a skull and an entire skeleton of a horse, because he would begin a painting from the bone structure. Thanks to my grandfather, I know horses inside and out. Crawling up and down and around and through them was lots of fun, but I never got really excited about being on top of them as a kid—although they got pretty excited when I crawled up and around them, especially those geldings!

We have two Icelandic horses whose names are not pronounceable so we call them Bob and Candy. A close friend's cousin, who is Icelandic, had them brought in from Iceland especially for us. Bob and Candy are a bit smaller than non-Icelandic horses. I look very funny sitting on them; I'm just under six-four so my feet hang down to their knees. While riding him bareback, Bob has thrown me a few times—but since I'm long and he's short, it's more like just rolling over in the grass.

Bob is a gelding and Candy is a mare. They get very hairy during the winter, but then again, so do I. Actually they get all fuzzy and grow long sort of "feathers"—a lot like golden retrievers. They're real skittish horses. . . . Hold on a minute, I've got two daughters and a wife yelling at me. My wife, Jayni, just told me that they are not skittish

at all but are very sure-footed and have a gait called a tolt, during which the horse lifts each foot independently. Tolting is amazing to watch and to ride. A fast tolt is very smooth so there's no need to post up and down.

Our property in Bedford is about fifteen acres, but we don't have a barn so the horses stay in my room. Actually, the facilities are fantastic. Bob and Candy's stalls are right next to each other, and we have rather sumptuous paddocks that they go out into during the day. Sometimes Bob and Candy frolic and other times they act about as bright as an egg timer. Once, several winters ago, I lost them in the woods. They just started going and going and were too excited by everything they saw to stop. I had to call one of the guys who works around here to help me hunt them down. When we found them I had to talk to them in a certain way and do some coaxing with a piece of bread so they would come back. They were gone long enough to get frostbite. Or was it me who got frostbite? Anyway . . .

"BOB AND CANDY ARE A BIT SMALLER THAN NON-ICELANDIC HORSES. I LOOK VERY FUNNY SITTING ON THEM."

Bedford is a gigantic horse area and boasts extensive riding trails. All three of my daughters ride, but Caley, who attends New York University, is the most accomplished. She and Candy have a wonderful connection. Both horses usually go out on the trails together, with Caley on Candy and Jayni on Bob. Jayni and Caley actually placed third in 2002 in Bedford's annual horse event, called the Pace, during which riders have to get to certain points in a specific amount of time. It's all about timing—what isn't?—and they go flying around the course really fast and very smoothly.

Being out here in the country, mucking out the stalls and cleaning up the poop, makes me much more laid back because I'm not getting paid to perform. As a matter of fact, I was up at four this morning cleaning Bob and Candy's stalls and feeding them. I'm not much more around here than a valet, chauffeur, and stable hand for my wife and three daughters—and I love it that way!

ROBERT DUVALL

From Lonesome Dove to Open Range

ACADEMY AWARD—WINNING ACTOR ROBERT DUVALL HAS STARRED AS SOME OF THE MOST MEMORABLE AND COMPELLING CHARACTERS ON BOTH THE BIG AND SMALL SCREENS. PERHAPS BEST KNOWN FOR HIS ACADEMY AWARD—NOMINATED ROLE AS THE FAMILY LAWYER IN *The Godfather* MOVIES, DUVALL WON HIS BEST ACTOR OSCAR IN 1983 FOR *Tender Mercies*, AND HE CEMENTED HIS REPUTATION AS ONE OF OUR FINEST ACTORS WITH HIS WORK IN *The Great Santini, Apocalypse Now, The Conversation,* AND *Rambling Rose*. ONE OF HIS GREATEST PROFESSIONAL TRIUMPHS, HOWEVER, WAS HIS PRODUCTION OF *The Apostle*, A POW-

ERFUL TALE OF A FALLEN SOUTHERN PREACHER WHO EVENTUALLY FINDS REDEMPTION. DUVALL ALSO WROTE AND DIRECTED THE MOVIE.

CELEBRATING A FORTY-YEAR CAREER, DUVALL'S FIRST RUN AT WESTERNS WAS ON THE *Stoney Burke* TELEVISION SERIES IN THE EARLY 1960s. HIS LATER WESTERN MOVIES INCLUDED *Lawman, True Grit*, AND *The Great Northfield Minnesota Raid*. IN 1989, HE MADE TELEVISION HISTORY BY STARRING AS AUGUSTUS MCCRAE IN THE HUGELY SUCCESSFUL, MULTI-AWARD-WINNING MINISERIES *Lonesome Dove*. HE ALSO PLAYED THE TITLE ROLE AND WON A GOLDEN GLOBE AWARD FOR BEST ACTOR IN THE HBO ORIGINAL FILM *Stalin*. AND IN 2001, DUVALL WENT TO ARGENTINA TO DIRECT, PRODUCE, AND STAR IN *Assassination Tango*, FOR WHICH HE ALSO WROTE THE SCRIPT. MOST RECENTLY, DUVALL STARRED IN 2003 AS THE SURPRISINGLY COMPASSIONATE BOSS IN THE CRITICALLY ACCLAIMED *Open Range* WITH KEVIN COSTNER.

DUVALL AND HIS PARTNER, LUCIANA PEDRAZA, LIVE IN A 1743 FARMHOUSE IN THE HILL COUNTRY OF VIRGINIA, WHERE SOME OF THE MOST ACCOMPLISHED GRAND PRIX RIDERS IN THE NATION RESIDE. BOTH THE REVOLUTIONARY AND CIVIL WARS WERE FOUGHT AROUND THIS FABULOUS PROPERTY, AND DUVALL'S MOTHER WAS A DISTANT RELATIVE OF ROBERT E. LEE, A ROLE HE ELOQUENTLY PLAYED IN THE 2003 TED TURNER FILM *Gods and Generals*.

I was introduced to horses at my

uncle's ranch in Montana, and that experience gave me the riding foundation to play in all the Westerns I've done over the years. I knew that for my first Western role, as a rodeo rider in the television series *Stoney Burke*, I should work at developing some sort of a seat. Back then in Hollywood, almost everyone working in movies could draw a gun, but no one knew how to sit properly on a horse. So I went to a rental stable in the Bronx to learn how to do it right.

After I moved to LA, I went to the Pickwick Riding Stables in the San Fernando Valley—now it's called the LA Equestrian Center—and started to ride in all three disciplines: bareback, Western, and English. I did that every day for two years straight and then landed a nice part in *True Grit*. That was back in the late sixties and early seventies, and I spent the next several years riding both English and Western with some wonderful trainers.

Then in 1988 I started training in earnest for *Lonesome Dove*. Around that time I even went to the beautiful farm of the great American jumping-horse rider Rodney Jenkins to

hone my skills, and he let me ride around his personal race-track.

There has been nothing to compare to starring in that movie. I know it sounds corny, but I always say, "Let the English play Hamlet or King Lear, I'll play Augustus McCrae." It was my favorite part ever. He was such a great character. I had lunch with Ann Richards, the ex-governor of Texas, and told her that I could run for governor and beat her—and she agreed that I probably could because *Lonesome Dove* is so popular down there.

Anyway, I did most of my own riding in that project. My main mount was a Running Quarter Horse that sometimes got a little bit too excited, so the wranglers found me a nice, calm animal from down South that was used in certain scenes. I was on one horse that started to buck like crazy when squibs (blanks) were fired, and the director actually used that footage in the movie. I was really in shape during that time and was riding pretty well.

After that, I got away from riding for a while. I had several quite serious falls, including one that was similar to what happened to Christopher Reeve. I flipped over a Dutch warmblood's neck onto my head. I probably had a minor concussion, but I rode in a local horse show several days later anyway. I named that horse Fino, after the best tango dancer I'd ever seen. Fino was a very good jumping horse, but I would also take him cross-country riding up and down hills just to keep us both fit. I sold him for a fortune and a year later he won a big Grand Prix over in Ireland.

But when Kevin Costner called me up and asked me to play this absolutely marvelous character in *Open Range*, I had to get back into riding. I played a trail boss who was right up

ABOVE: THEY HAVE TWO BARNS ON THEIR 360 ACRES.

LEFT: DECOR IN THEIR BARN INCLUDES A COLORFUL CURTAIN MADE OF WINNING RIBBONS AND A DISPLAY OF "BITS"

"PERHAPS IF I HADN'T GONE INTO ACTING I'D BE A RANCHER SOMEPLACE OUT WEST."

there with Augustus McCrae as far as parts go. I hadn't ridden that much in years, and going up to Canada with six broken ribs that were still healing from another accident I'd had was a little tiffy. But luckily they had very good cowboys up there, and the producers found me a good horse. There's a really great scene where I drive some horses up a hill at a canter. Fifteen years ago I would have done that scene in my sleep and it would not have been at all challenging, so it felt particularly rewarding to be able to do that again.

My uncle always said I was a natural on a horse, and perhaps if I hadn't gone into acting I'd be a rancher someplace out

West. Luciana, too, used to show horses in northern Argentina. But where we're living now, in Virginia horse and hill country, you have to be pretty modest when you state that you are a horseman. There are true world-class riders in this area. Katie Monahan Prudent lives around here, jumping legend Rodney Jenkins lives down state, and David O'Connor, who won the gold medal at the Olympics in Three Day Eventing, is from this county.

Willy, the horse that we have here now, came from South Carolina. I rode him in the movie *Something to Talk About*, and I brought him back here after the movie was finished shooting. He's been here ever since. We used to jump him during filming there in the sand, which had a lot of traction and slowed him down, but when he got up here there was not much sand, and he tended to take off. He's an older horse now but still very athletic and beautiful. Luciana didn't expect much when she rode him in competition for the first time, as he is not really a hunter, but she won a blue ribbon at that show.

I love to watch Grand Prix jumping, and a great young rider who I have been following is Aaron Vail, who doubled for me in *Something to Talk About*. He jumped the whole course in the movie with one hand on the reins and the other one holding a handheld camera. I also enjoy watching the hunt that goes through our property sometimes. It's kind of an unwritten law that you can jump a fence or come onto private grounds if you need to in pursuit of the fox. Our farm is more than 250 years old, so I'm sure that hundreds of horses have ridden across these fields.

While we don't do as much pleasure riding as we used to, Luciana and I do think about getting some old bomb-proof Quarter Horses and bringing them out here. When you get on a horse and go nice and easy across country it makes you feel really good, it definitely does. I remember that great saying about horses from Winston Churchill: "There is something about the outside of a horse that is good for the inside of a man."

RICHARD GERE

At Home with Appaloosas

ACTOR RICHARD GERE IS KNOWN NOT ONLY AS ONE OF HOLLY-WOOD'S MOST CHARISMATIC LEADING MEN, BUT ALSO AS A DEDI-CATED SOCIAL ACTIVIST AND HUMAN RIGHTS ADVOCATE WHO HAS EMBRACED SUCH CAUSES AS THE ONGOING SEARCH FOR A CURE FOR AIDS AND CHAMPIONED SURVIVAL AND FREEDOM FOR THE PEOPLE OF TIBET.

GERE BEGAN HIS ACTING CAREER IN 1975 AND GAVE A MESMERIZING PERFORMANCE OPPOSITE DIANE KEATON IN *Looking for Mr. Goodbar* IN 1977. THE NEXT YEAR, HE STARRED IN THE BREATHTAKINGLY BEAUTIFUL MOVIE *Days of Heaven*, AND THE VERSATILE ACTOR WAS OFF ON A TWO-AND-A-HALF-DECADE STREAK OF MEMORABLE ROLES: IN *American Gigolo*, *An Officer and a Gentleman*, *Internal Affairs*, *Sommersby*, *Primal Fear*, AND, OF COURSE, *Pretty Woman* AND *Runaway Bride* OPPOSITE JULIA ROBERTS. GERE STARRED WITH DIANE LANE IN *Unfaithful* IN 2002, AND LATER THAT YEAR HE STRUCK GOLD WITH HIS AWARD-WINNING PERFORMANCE IN *Chicago*, WHICH GARNERED HIM A GOLDEN GLOBE AWARD FOR BEST ACTOR.

GERE AND HIS WIFE, ACTRESS CAREY LOWELL, WHO IS BEST KNOWN FOR HER YEARS ON THE POPULAR NBC TELEVISION SERIES *Law & Order*, SHARE A PASSION FOR THEIR BEAUTIFUL APPALOOSA HORSES. THEY ARE BOTH SUPPORTERS OF THE CHIEF JOSEPH FOUN-DATION, WHICH FOCUSES ON NEZ PERCE CULTURAL PRESERVATION, EMPHASIZING KIDS PROGRAMS WITH AND AROUND THEIR AP-PALOOSAS. (THE FOUNDATION CAN BE REACHED AT 208-843-7175.) THE FAMILY LIVES ON A BEAUTIFUL HORSE PROPERTY IN NEW YORK WITH THEIR FOUR APPALOOSAS, TWO CHILDREN, TWO CATS, AND A DOG.

"I first became aware of Appaloosas

in the late 1970s when I was doing Sam Shepard's one-act play *Killer's Head* off Broadway. I played a rodeo guy who's blindfolded and strapped in an electric chair. During his rambling parting interior monologue, he goes on about pickup trucks, Colorado, and Appaloosas.

Appaloosas were bred by the Nez Perce tribes of Oregon, Washington, and Idaho, and were probably the first selectively bred horses in the Americas. The Nez Perce bred them for their stamina, for their extraordinary, expressionistic coloring, and for their easy temperament. They have very human eyes.

"The Nez Perce, mounted on their spectral Appaloosas, were the finest light cavalry in the world. They were also one of the last Native American tribes that the U.S.

Army was able to defeat. Just miles from the Canadian border at Bear Paw, Montana, Chief Joseph surrendered in 1877. Many of the Nez Perce were killed and their horses systematically slaughtered to destroy them as a fighting force. A few of these magnificent animals were stolen by the soldiers, and some others escaped into the mountains. These were the foundation stock of the breed we know today.

"My horse Drukpa came from the rodeo circuit, and I couldn't ask for a finer animal, or a horse more suited to me. Carey's horse, Kali, is a stunning black mare, with a perfect white blanket on her butt. Her bloodline goes back to Secretariat. Apparently, she caused a lot of roadside accidents back in Idaho. Drivers would see her and slam on their brakes to get a better look. I got Kali from Bonnie and Bill Ewing. Bonnie is a board member of the Chief Joseph Foundation. In 1991, a breeder from New Mexico donated some of his Appaloosa stock to help form the Chief Joseph Foundation. The Foundation's focus is on Nez Perce cultural preservation, emphasizing programs with and around their Appaloosas. It reintroduces the youth of the Nez Perce to their ancient horse culture and away from drugs, alcohol, and despair. I am very happy to be helping them out and would recommend everyone else do the same."

"Richard and I had been helping the Foundation and were looking for a horse," says Carey, "so we drove up to Idaho and came back with a mare who was really kind of unridable. She was basically a beautiful horse who was used to being treated as a pet—always looking for her treats. But she's turned out great. We didn't have her long before she was with foal, and Jigme was born. He is dark with no markings on his body, just a white star on his forehead—not very Appaloosa, but he's smart and athletic. He's going to be our son's horse. Before I met Richard, I didn't know how special they were, or their history as a Native American breed. But most appealing are their big hearts. They will do anything you ask them to do."

"Another great trait of the Appaloosa is that they calm down very quickly," continues Richard. "I can get a little crazy, running the horses through the woods and jumping them, but they calm right down. This big Appy follows me around like a dog. He had some leg problems when I first got him. He was used as a turn-back horse at a rodeo in Saratoga, New York. (A turn-back horse helps get other horses and livestock back into the pens during a rodeo.) I bought him sight unseen on the recommendation of my friends Eddie Parchment and Andrea Eastman. He's my first horse. First horses are like your first girlfriend. You never forget. He's very athletic and very fast. We've taken good care of each other

"BUT MOST APPEALING ARE THEIR BIG HEARTS. THEY WILL DO ANYTHING YOU ASK THEM TO DO."

"THE FIRST RIDES THAT CAREY AND I TOOK TOGETHER WERE UP HERE IN THE WINTER. WONDERFUL FRESH SNOW ON MILES AND MILES OF TRAILS."

over the years. It's in the breed. He'd run his heart out for me. I just love him. He's almost twenty-three now, and we just re-tired him. He just eats and sleeps and plays with his friend Kali. Not a bad life.

"I got him as an eight year old just before I did the film *Somersby* and brought him down to Virginia where we were

shooting. The production had built a Civil War-era town in the middle of a national forest, complete with fields and a stable. So, I just left Drukpa in the paddock there. When I had a ten-minute break, I just saddled him up and took off! It was a perfect situation.

"The horse I rode in *First Knight* was another terrific horse, an Andalusian. A very proud breed. I'd seen the horse first on tape, being ridden by this extraordinary Spanish rider, using no bridle and with his hands clasped behind his back. Voice and leg commands only. Unbelievably sensitive. He was far too good for me, and it took quite a while for me to ride him properly. That horse taught me a lot.

"I'd always liked horses, although I didn't ride much growing up. My father grew up on a dairy farm in Pennsyl-vania and they really didn't have riding horses, but he would tell me stories about the farm mules and horses pulling the plow. My mother's father did have a riding horse and I do re-member riding him. Named Hale, I think. I was intrigued but a little afraid of the animals on the farm. I remember being treed by a herd of milk cows one whole afternoon when I was a kid. I didn't really learn to ride until I got this place up here eighteen years ago.

"The first rides that Carey and I took together were up here in the winter. Wonderful fresh snow on miles and miles of trails. She was fearless and I thought, 'Man, this girl's for me.'"

MELISSA GILBERT AND BRUCE BOXLEITNER

The Ties That Bind

MELISSA GILBERT LITERALLY GREW UP BEFORE MILLIONS OF AR-DENT VIEWERS IN THE ROLE OF LAURA INGALLS ON THE TELEVISION SERIES *Little House on the Prairie*. IT WAS AT THE OLD BIG SKY MOVIE RANCH NORTH OF LOS ANGELES, WHERE THE SERIES WAS FILMED, THAT GILBERT STARTED TO RIDE OFF-CAMERA AT THE AGE OF NINE. FOR HER STARRING ROLE IN *Sylvester*, TRULY THE STORY OF A GIRL AND HER HORSE, GILBERT DID MOST OF HER OWN STUNT WORK AND RODE EIGHT HOURS A DAY. RELISHING ROLES IN CLASSIC

HORSES. PERHAPS BEST KNOWN FOR HIS STARRING ROLES IN THE URBAN COMEDY SERIES *Scarecrow & Mrs. King* AND THE SCIENCE FICTION DRAMA SERIES *Babylon 5*. BOXLEITNER ALSO ACTED IN MANY WESTERNS, FROM THE REMAKE OF *Red River* AND *Louis L'Amour's Down the Long Hills* TO THE 2003 *Gods and Generals*.

GILBERT AND BOXLEITNER BOTH RETREATED TO THE HORSE COMMUNITY OF HIDDEN HILLS, JUST THIRTY-FIVE MILES NORTH OF LOS ANGELES, IN THE LATE 1970S AND THE LATE 1980S, RESPEC-

REMAKES, SHE HAS STARRED IN *The Miracle Worker*, *The Diary of Anne Frank*, *Splendor in the Grass*, AND, MOST RECENTLY, *The Soul Collector* AND *Switched at Birth*. GILBERT IS ALSO THE PRES-IDENT OF THE SCREEN ACTORS GUILD, A POSITION THAT KEEPS HER VERY BUSY.

LIFE ALSO IMITATED ART FOR BRUCE BOXLEITNER, WHOSE FIRST BIG ACTING ROLE WAS AS JAMES ARNESS'S NEPHEW IN THE TV MINISERIES *How the West Was Won*, WHICH WAS FILMED IN UTAH, ARIZONA, AND COLORADO, AS WELL AS IN SOUTHERN CAL-IFORNIA. DURING THE SHOOTING, BOXLEITNER FELL IN LOVE WITH

TIVELY, WHILE MARRIED TO OTHER PEOPLE. BOXLEITNER HAD FALLEN IN LOVE WITH THE AREA WHILE FILMING *How the West Was Won* AND PURCHASED A SMALL RANCH AS SOON AS HE COULD AFFORD IT. A DECADE LATER, GILBERT MOVED TO HIDDEN HILLS AND BECAME INVOLVED WITH BOTH TRAINING AND RIDING WESTERN TRAIL HORSES.

IN 1993, BOXLEITNER BEGAN COURTING GILBERT ON HORSE-BACK. AFTER MORE THAN A YEAR OF BACKYARD LEMONADE AND COOKIES, AS WELL AS LATE-AFTERNOON RIDES, THE COUPLE WENT TO THE HITCHING POST IN 1995.

"There was this amazing moment

when Bruce and I first started dating about ten years ago," says Melissa Gilbert, reminiscing about an early encounter with her husband, Bruce Boxleitner. "We were out riding through the Ahmanson Ranch in the most western part of the San Fernando Valley. We were sitting on our horses looking out at the vista of the Valley, the lighted sky was turning gold, and I kept thinking that this must have been how magical it was for such actors as Clark Gable and Carol Lombard who were here more than fifty years before Bruce and I were.

"I immediately keyed in on this visual of them sitting on their horses and how lucky Bruce and I were to be part of that legacy of people who can go riding and explore the undeveloped splendor of Los Angeles. It was so magnificent to be able to see how this country used to be. Sitting there and looking at Bruce, I remember thinking, 'We are here.'"

"I actually started courting Melissa on horseback," says Bruce. "We both lived in Hidden Hills, about a mile or two away from each other, and I was single and she was going through a divorce, so I would just saddle up and ride by her house. Melissa had a nice little barn and corral and two great horses, and I would ride by and call out 'Hello!' and she would come out on the balcony and say, 'Come on in!' My horse, Jake, and I would ride onto her property and I would loosen his cinch and tether him to the hitching rail. It gave me a very old-fashioned feeling, like out of *Little House on the Prairie*."

"Bruce was this big old handsome cowboy on that beautiful horse," gushes Melissa.

"Melissa had animals everywhere, and her seven dogs—give or take one or two—would maul me, and then we would go

riding together. I rarely drove to her house unless we were going out on an actual date. It seemed kind of romantic that way."

"He would hitch up his horse and come into the house for ice tea or lemonade and we would ride together, and then we would come home and have dinner and hang out with our kids, and then he would ride home."

Since that time the couple has spent many pleasurable hours together on horseback.

Melissa learned to ride when she started acting in *Little*

to take away her brothers, and Charlie, played by me, decides that if she can prove that breaking horses is a real job, she can keep her family together. So Charlie takes this big, old, untrained bucking cow horse and decides to train him and sell him to the Olympic Equestrian Team.

"In this movie I did most of the riding and had to learn how to do everything from herding cattle to cross-country eventing and stadium jumping. My legs were so bruised—I rode six hours a day, six days a week. It was so amazing riding this fabulous Appaloosa while chasing another horse on a highway next to a camera car going forty-five miles an hour. This was definitely a stunt that I wouldn't do now!

"Sylvester, the horse, and I trained at the same time. He had never jumped before, and neither had I. He tried to throw me off of him; he ran off with me and tried everything that he could do to get me off of his back. It was a battle of wills from the beginning, and there was no way one of us was going to dominate the other. The training was a remarkable eight weeks long and my trainer really put me through the paces. By the time we had finished, I could do a whole circuit of dressage in the arena without reins, just using my legs. This was not a horse that I would have chosen to have in my life, but we had no choice other than to get along and to make the relationship work, and we did."

Bruce admits that it was the romantic image of the West that had a hold on him. "I always wanted to live the cowboy lifestyle. When I moved to Southern California and landed *How the West Was Won*, it was a dream come true for me. There was a new version of the classic film in development at Warner Brothers and I was cast as James Arness's nephew. Here I was, out in Utah, out on horseback playing in a Western. I got to know all the horse people on the show, like the wranglers who had worked with

House at the age of nine, although she didn't ride much on the show. "Off-camera I would beg to ride and the wranglers would throw me up on my show horse, Peewee, and send me off with the stuntmen. After *Little House* ended I was afraid that I was going to have to mourn the passing of my former life with horses. But then *Sylvester* came along. It was the true story of a sixteen-year-old orphan named Charlie from Texas who is raising her two brothers and working for a man who breaks horses, played by Richard Farnsworth. The state comes

"INDEED, JUST AS THERE ARE POWERFUL TIES THAT BIND A MAN AND WOMAN TOGETHER, THERE IS A SPECIAL KIND OF TRUST THAT OFTEN DEVELOPS IN MAN'S—AND WOMAN'S—RELATIONSHIP WITH A HORSE."

horses for generations in the movie business. It was a great show, but more importantly it introduced me to my lifelong dream of working and living around horses. We used to shoot out here not two miles from where I live, in Malibu Canyon at Malibu State Park, which was not a state park then but a movie ranch. We also went on location and shot in Utah, Colorado, Arizona, and even to Bend, Oregon, for part of an episode."

Along the way, Bruce's desire to buy a horse got stronger and stronger. Then he discovered a horse-friendly community called Hidden Hills where he could commit to the whole Western lifestyle. "That smell of horses and livestock just took me back to my childhood and the time spent on my grandfather's farm. Just having big animals around was something I dove into. I found one of those little 1950s-style ranch houses and got busy building and repairing fences. I really enjoy that kind of work." Bruce would even ride from his house through a tunnel under the Ventura Freeway to the Calabasas Saloon, tie up his horse, go inside for a drink, and then ride home.

Ultimately, Bruce was able to buy one of the horses he rode in *How the West Was Won*, Old 55, which he named after a song by the band the Eagles. "Many years later I donated Old 55 to this wonderful horse organization called Ahead with Horses where disabled children get to ride. My next horse was Socks, a dapple gray about sixteen hands tall, and I used to charge all over the place on him. But I do have to say that my two favorites were my roping horses Brownie and Jake. As big and gangly as he looked, Jake was really very nimble and fast. He was one of those horses that I could step down from, drop the reins, and walk away and he would still be there an hour later when I came back. He was the best of the best. His prior history was that he had been a rodeo champ and had won the Cow Palace All-Around in San Francisco. He was just a tremendous athlete, and, boy, did Melissa and I cry when he eventually passed away."

"Jake was, I think, the greatest horse that either of us have ever owned," agrees Melissa. "He was so patient, strong, and kind. Nothing bothered him. I would trust my children's lives with that horse."

Indeed, just as there are powerful ties that bind a man and woman together, there is a special kind of trust that often develops in man's—and woman's—relationship with a horse. Says Melissa, "We recently went to see *The Lord of the Rings: The Two Towers*, and I started to cry when I saw Gandolf riding that white horse. For some reason that majestic animal ripped my heart out."

She adds, "We have ridden horses into battle, we've ridden them for transportation through the wilderness, and we've used them to plow our fields. In return, they depend on us for feeding, loving, and grooming. It's an interdependence of trust, and it's truly something special."

RIGHT: BRUCE AND MELISSA AT DIRECTOR MARTHA COOLIDGE'S RANCH IN SOUTHERN CALIFORNIA. THE BEAUTIFUL FOAL IS JUST ONE MONTH OLD.

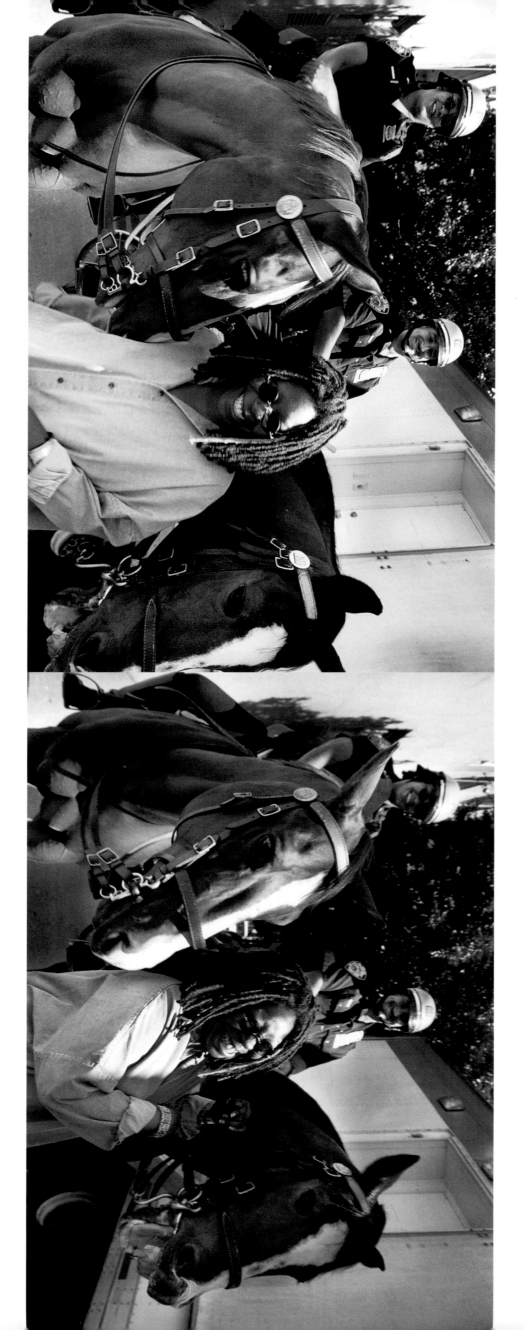

WHOOOPI GOLDBERG

In 2002, Whoopi Goldberg became one of a very very elite group of artists who have won the Grammy, the Academy Award, the Golden Globe, the Emmy, and the Tony. After her stellar Broadway debut in her one-woman *The Spook Show*, Goldberg made her film debut in Steven Spielberg's *The Color Purple*, garnering the Golden Globe and an Oscar nomination. In 1991, Goldberg won another Golden Globe and the Oscar for her performance in *Ghost* and she's gone on to star in dozens of feature films and television projects.

Having also made her mark behind the scenes, Goldberg currently stars in her own NBC comedy series, aptly titled just plain *Whoopi*, which she also executive produces.

As a young girl, Goldberg fell in love with the horses of the New York City Mounted Police. She recently sold her horse property in upstate Connecticut, not realizing how much she would miss her four horses. They all went to good homes in the area, but she is now actively looking for thirty acres in the country, where she can once again return to a lifestyle that has given her so much happiness in the past.

Goldberg was photographed on the streets of New York with Yvette Anderson and Anthony Oliveri from the NYPD Mounted Police Troop F.

The Horses of New York

I grew up in the projects in Chelsea,

New York. My first experience with horses was when I went to Central Park and would see the mounted police officers on their mounts. It was like having a slice of the country in the city. The horses always looked so tall, proud, and beautiful trotting up Ninth Avenue—there was nothing more beautiful. Their hooves made such a distinctive sound clattering on the street. Frequently when I was riding on a bus, a mounted policeman would ride along next to the old bus windows, smiling and nodding at you. I would nod back and he would clop off with that great sound. Soon I got just silly over police horses—I would pet them and ask the officers all kinds of questions. Those officers were always there, and, even now, if kids come around them they will talk about their horses and what they can do. They are really doing a great thing for the city.

One of the great visuals in television history is of Dennis Weaver as McCloud galloping through the streets of New York complete with cowboy hat and shearling coat. McCloud is a show that I would loved to have done. I would play a cowboy in a minute. I've ridden in two Disney movies, A Connecticut Yankee in King Arthur's Court and Golden Dreams, which plays at California Adventure, and my dream would be to star in a remake of The Magnificent Seven. I would love to play a woman cowboy who was passing herself off as a man.

The horses and carriages at Central Park also made a great impression on me. The carriage drivers would smile at you as they were picking up tourists from around those swank hotels. There were also two equestrian centers at the Park, in the middle of Manhattan, but it never did occur to me and my friends to go riding there.

I never had horses growing up, but when I started to become successful I bought a place in Connecticut and had four horses there. My absolute favorite was an unridable black stallion named Shadow who had a giant apparatus. Shadow was a short

horse, and in order to breed him, the mare had to be put in a hole so she could accept him when he unfolded. This type of mating didn't really work very well, so my friends and family and I came to the conclusion that Shadow really shouldn't be bred. He was so beautiful and proud and no one but me could ride him because he would try and buck everyone else off of his back. My favorite thing to do was just getting on his back and walking through my property. A lot of people love the thrill of galloping through their riding area, but I loved to take it nice and slow on Shadow. Historically, this is the way that people used to travel—not in such a rush. You're just moving forward, you and the animal. Shadow and I would have some carrots, a cube of sugar, and a bottle of water, and we were both very, very happy.

"MY FIRST EXPERIENCE WITH HORSES WAS WHEN I WENT TO CENTRAL PARK AND WOULD SEE THE MOUNTED POLICE OFFICERS ON THEIR MOUNTS. IT WAS LIKE HAVING A SLICE OF THE COUNTRY IN THE CITY."

In a sense, my horses have kept me centered. Several years ago I started to put on some weight. It used to be very easy for me to mount Shadow, even bareback, because I had a mounting box and could hoist myself up on his back. But one day, I just couldn't get up on Shadow's back no matter how hard I tried. I tried every jump known to mankind and just could not get up on that horse. Fifteen minutes later, I

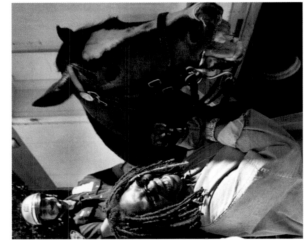

gave the horse two carrots and a sugar cube and realized that I was carrying too much weight to be comfortable on him and decided to do something about it.

It was a mistake to have sold that property, but it was two-and-a-half hours away from New York, and if I had a meeting at my house it would cost people a whole day to get there. But I do miss my horses and am looking for some great horse property in the country. I want at least thirty acres and will definitely have horses again. It's a wonderful thing to look out of your window and see them grazing. I just love it when their lips start to move and the upper one comes out just a bit. Shadow would start moving those lips and then he would move his mouth up the back of my neck and grab my hair. They look at you oddly sometimes, and you wonder what they are thinking about you. Are they thinking, "You look ridiculous"?

"WHEN I GET ON A HORSE IT CAN REDUCE THE EVENTS IN MY LIFE TO A SIMPLE DESIRE TO STAY ALIVE," SAYS GRAMMER.

KELSEY AND CAMILLE GRAMMER

Sharing a Life Together with Horses

THE NAMES KELSEY GRAMMER AND DR. FRASIER CRANE HAVE BECOME INTERCHANGEABLE DURING A REMARKABLE TWENTY-YEAR RUN OF HIGH-QUALITY TELEVISION. AS DR. CRANE, A PSYCHIATRIST WHO OUTWARDLY SEEMED VERY WELL ADJUSTED BUT INTERNALLY WAS IN DESPERATE NEED OF THE COUCH HIMSELF, GRAMMER STARRED IN THE HIT NBC COMEDY *Cheers* FOR ALMOST A DECADE. HE WON HIS FIRST EMMY AWARD FOR BEST LEAD ACTOR IN A COMEDY SERIES IN 1993 REPRISING HIS ROLE OF DR. CRANE IN *Frasier*, AND OVER THE NEXT SEVEN YEARS HE RECEIVED TWO ADDITIONAL EMMY AWARDS AND TWO GOLDEN GLOBE AWARDS. HE TIED WITH RAY ROMANO (*Everybody Loves Raymond*) FOR THE PEOPLE'S CHOICE AWARD FAVORITE MALE TELEVISION PERFORMER IN 2002, ALL FOR HIS CLASSIC FRASIER CRANE CHARACTER.

AND YES, SUCCESS DOES HAVE ITS REWARDS. GRAMMER AND HIS BEAUTIFUL WIFE CAMILLE NOW LIVE ON A SIXTEEN-ACRE MALIBU ESTATE SURROUNDED BY THE HORSES THEY LOVE. THE PROPERTY HAS A FULL STABLE, TACK ROOM, AND RIDING RING AND IS A TRUE RETREAT FROM THE RIGORS OF A MORE-THAN-FULL-TIME TELEVISION CAREER. BOTH ARE THOROUGHBRED LOVERS. KELSEY'S FAVORITE HORSE IS THE MAJESTIC SEVENTEEN-HAND NAPOLEON, WHILE CAMILLE RIDES THE MORE ELEGANT SOX. THE COUPLE ALSO LOVES THE FORM OF THE HORSE, AND A TOWERING HORSE SCULPTURE AND REGAL MARBLE HORSE FOUNTAIN CAN BE FOUND ON THEIR WANDERING MOUNTAINTOP PROPERTY.

For Kelsey and Camille Grammer,

spending time with their horses in Malibu is a welcome way to escape the high-intensity glare of Hollywood. "I don't know how well I fit into that scene per se," says Kelsey, "and so our home is our refuge. We come here to hang out. Camille and I both love the property, the horses, and the outdoor lifestyle. When I get on a horse it can reduce the events in my life to a simple desire to stay alive."

"The air is so fresh and the area so beautiful and pristine," agrees Camille. "There were already horses here when I first discovered this property, and we decided to buy it because we knew these amazing animals would be such a plus. The house needed lots of work, but that was okay with us. Now the barn is almost full of beautiful horses, and we have become regular riders over the last several years."

Kelsey remembers how even just the sight of horses helped put him at ease. "When we first bought our property, the horses that were already there and the equine facilities were wonderful to look at. They had such a visual charm about them. The whole scene conjured up a peaceful and pastoral quality, which was something I could use in my life, coming from what I call the concrete desolation of Los Angeles. Then we discovered that we really could learn how to ride, and we grabbed the opportunity by buying Sox and Napoleon."

"We actually call them our big dogs," says Camille. "We would keep them in the house if it were possible."

Kelsey's horse Napoleon, it turns out, had been a great competitor. But he had one major flaw: he was afraid of water. "Napoleon was devalued as a hunter-jumper, but he was and is of great value to me. What I have is a great athlete who is a little bit temperamental. He is also afraid of his own shadow, which is an interesting phenomenon. The first time I came around a corner sitting on Napoleon and the sun was directly behind him, he saw his shadow and really spooked. But the good thing about my relationship with Napoleon is that he is basically teaching me how to ride him. I have done some jumping, too, although I am certainly not skilled at the sport, and Napoleon helps me with that at his discretion."

Kelsey says that his appreciation of horses goes back to his childhood days and is a form of homage to his grandfather. "I was brought up by my granddad, who was raised on a ranch in California. He was never a roping and steer-throwing kind of a guy, but he was a

"RIDING CLEARS THE HEAD, LEVELS YOU, AND GETS YOU IN SYNC WITH SOMETHING ELSE THAT IS BREATHING AND MOVING."

great rider and knew what it meant to live that simple code. There is something true about doing the right thing and having simple values that embody what it means to be a cowboy." It's those values, along with the sheer pleasure of riding, that first caught the young Kelsey's fancy. "When I was a young boy, I started riding on a giant seventeen-hand Palomino at camp and thought that this was the greatest thing ever."

As often happens with childhood enthusiasms, Kelsey got away from riding for many years before returning to the saddle later in life. By then, he found the experience slightly different than he'd remembered. "I started riding again about five-and-a-half years ago, and it turned out to be much greater physical exercise than I ever anticipated, and a mental challenge as well. It's a lot harder to ride—to ride well—than people think it is, especially if you are training and jumping in the riding ring. My posterior and various

other parts around that area initially took a real physical beating—if you know what I mean."

But despite the sore spots, he revels in the challenge and feeds off the feelings that being on a horse inspire. "Riding clears the head, levels you, and gets you in sync with some-thing else that is breathing and moving. You have to be very careful about what you are doing, but riding relaxes you, gets those endorphins moving. And there is something wonderful about taking care of animals. It gets you in touch with some kind of life force. I truly look forward to riding after work and on weekends, and I really want to ride a horse in a movie someday!"

At this point, Camille can't resist talking up her own horse, Sox. "Just off the kitchen there's a little outside living area with a table and chairs, and I just love eating with Sox. We walk up the driveway to the kitchen, I give him an apple, and we have lunch together."

"I find that a little alarming, but at least it isn't another man," quips Kelsey. "But seriously, Camille's love of horses, and especially for Sox, has raised my estimation of her as a caring and loving person. She is so open to new ideas and experiences and is very physically fit. We've had some very memorable experiences on these horses—some exhilarating and some a little bit frightening. One of my most fun and amazing memories was when I put together a three-in-a-row jump for the first time. There was only one stride in between each jump and it was almost like flying!"

"The peak experiences for me have also revolved around jumping," says Camille. "The first time was really incredible, as you truly do feel like you're flying and the horse does in fact take you slightly airborne. I also remember one particular day when Sox and I were in complete harmony. He is a Thoroughbred and has a beautiful fast trot, and one day the breeze was blowing and he started to step out, not even a canter, but I got into a two-point position and I felt that we were truly one. It was a transcendent experience for me."

Listening attentively to his partner, Kelsey relaxes into a smile. "It makes me so happy to see Camille enjoying herself like this. Our mutual love of horses has been one thing that we have been able to explore and enjoy together. Her way with horses makes me appreciate her even more. Every day I pinch myself. I am really happy."

15-FOOT-HIGH HORSE
SCULPTURE BY GEORGE LEZANO
FROM ROSARITO, MEXICO

JOE AND BILLIE PERRY

A Love Affair with Friesians

STILL INCREDIBLY HIP AFTER THIRTY OFF-AND-ON YEARS AS STAR GUITARIST IN THE MULTI GRAMMY AWARD–WINNING GROUP HE HELPED FOUND, AEROSMITH'S JOE PERRY HAS MADE HIS UNIQUE MARK ON MUSIC WITH SUCH ROCK CLASSICS AS "SWEET EMO-TION," "DREAM ON," "JANIE'S GOT A GUN," AND "ANGEL." WELL KNOWN FOR THE SPECTACULAR SHOW THEY PUT ON, PERRY AND THE REST OF THE BAND WOWED MIL-LIONS OF TELEVISION VIEWERS WHEN THEY PERFORMED THEIR MULTIGENERATIONAL HIT "WALK THIS WAY" WITH AN ALL-STAR GROUP THAT INCLUDED *NSYNC AND BRITNEY SPEARS AT THE 2002 SUPER BOWL HALFTIME SHOW. AND AEROSMITH'S 2002 TWO-CD COLLECTION O, Yeah! Ultimate Aerosmith Hits WENT PLATINUM IN JUST A MATTER OF WEEKS.

WHEN PERRY COMES OFF THE ROAD FOLLOWING A TRIUMPHANT BUT GRUELING WORLDWIDE TOUR, HE AND HIS WIFE, BILLIE, FIND CONTENTMENT AND RELAXATION WITH THEIR TWO FRIESIAN HORSES, ORIEN AND FRANZ, ON THEIR FARM NORTH OF BOSTON, WHERE AEROSMITH RECORDED ITS NEW BLUES ALBUM. JOE AND BILLIE HAVE HAD A FIFTEEN-YEAR LOVE AFFAIR WITH FRIESIANS. PERRY'S FIRST SIGNATURE-MODEL GUITAR, DESIGNED BY GIBSON AND INSPIRED BY FRIESIANS, IS NAMED ACCORDINGLY. AND WHEN BILLIE FIRST SAW A PHOTOGRAPH OF A MAJESTIC COAL-BLACK FRIESIAN, SHE KNEW INSTINCTIVELY THAT HERE WAS A HORSE FIT FOR A ROCK STAR. LIKE JOE, FRIESIANS HAVE A WONDERFUL SENSE OF ELEGANCE, SHE SAYS. SHE EVEN JOKES THAT JOE AND HIS BELOVED FRIESIANS LOOK REMARKABLY ALIKE! ONE THING'S FOR SURE: A GREAT DAY FOR THIS HORSE-LOVING COUPLE IS HANGING OUT AT THE STALLS AND LIS-TENING TO A LITTLE COUNTRY MUSIC IN FRONT OF THE WOODSTOVE WHILE ENJOYING THE COMPANY OF THEIR HORSES.

"Joe and I have always loved animals,"

says Billie Perry. "We've had just about every pet you can own, from Koi fish to dogs and even uninvited otters. So when we moved out of the city to what you would call the suburban countryside, we decided to get horses. That was back in 1987. I had ridden regularly growing up, but Joe had only ridden a couple of times. We bought a Quarter Horse and a Paint, and Joe fell in love with horses. We would get out horse encyclopedias and look through them and see all the beautiful photos of horses from around the world. There was one picture of the most fascinating looking horse that I had ever seen in my life. So I started to bait Joe by saying, 'Joe, this horse is so cool and it's all black. This is the perfect horse for you.'" Joe and Billie also recognized it as the breed of horse that starred in a movie they loved, *Ladyhawke*.

But the couple would soon find out that seeing a real live Friesian was much easier said than done.

"Friesians are big, black, beautiful, long-maned animals that were very rare in this country when we started our search," says Joe. "This was before the Internet, so it took Billie and I a while to see one in the flesh."

"We were on tour in Nashville in June 1990," Joe remembers, "and Billie was reading *Horse and Horseman* magazine. She found an article on world-class warmbloods, and next thing I know she's screaming, 'Oh my God, Joe, they're Friesians!'"

"There was an ad in the magazine for the Friesian Horse Association of North America, with a contact number for the man who was then the head of the club," says Billie.

Adds Joe, "You could count the stallions on one hand in this country way back then, so we got to know just about every line, as there were so few of them."

Friesians have a remarkable history as warhorses dating back to 1,000 B.C. They are the oldest registered breed in Holland, and that country's national horse. They are all

JOE AND BILLIE
WITH THEIR THREE
SONS, ROMAN, AGE
12; AARON
(SEATED), AGE 30;
AND TONY, AGE 17,
AND MINI HORSE

42

black and should not have any white on them at all, except for a small star on their head. If they have any white other than a star, they are disqualified from being considered purebred.

"At that point, in 1990, I don't think they had ever qualified a stallion born in this country," says Joe. "The judges come over from Holland and put the stallions through all the tests, including size, color, confirmation, and gait, among many others. Everyone is working to get the Dutch judges to qualify a stallion over here and it has been insane because they haven't been able to do it yet."

Billie adds that only a colt born from an approved stallion and approved mare is qualified to be a breeding Friesian stallion.

"The Dutch are so strict," she says, "because these horses almost became extinct. Friesians were originally used during medieval times as warhorses and then used as carriage horses, and after cars were introduced people used them to pull plows. They gradually started to die off and were not being bred much any more, and after World War II they were put on the endangered species list."

Joe is pleased to note that the breed is slowly starting to make a comeback. "Most people think that Friesians are for pulling a carriage and that kind of thing because they tend to be a larger-bodied horse like a Clydesdale or other draft. It takes even horse people a while to get used to the idea that they are great under saddle. When a Friesian finally competed in a national dressage show here in the East and won most events, it was a monumental accomplishment, because these horses weren't used in American dressage much due to the small numbers of horses available in the United States. The

fact that they are winning events in this country has made Friesians more popular."

Still, that wasn't the case back in the early 1990s, when tracking down leads on Friesians became a regular pursuit for Joe and Billie. While on tour with the band they would steal away to places that boasted of having these amazing horses. For instance, they visited a dairy farm in Southern California where the owner had Friesian stallions driving his restored 1800s carriage.

"Magnum was the horse that Joe rode for years," says Billie. And it was Magnum that hooked them on the breed. "Then we got Nico. Nico was very beautiful but also very fiery. He was a hot boy, and so huge that he looked like a sculpture right out of ancient Rome—you know, the warhorse with the big arch in the neck and the long mane. Our next Friesian, Orien, was two years old when we bought him. He was a half brother to Nico, and we have had him for thirteen years."

Their next Friesian, Franz, came into their lives after a chance meeting with a Danish breeder at a national equestrian show in Reno in 1999. "I told him this laundry list of what I wanted for Joe—the horse had to have a great temperament and traditional features," remembers Billie. "He said, 'I think I have the horse for you, but he is in Germany right now.' So he sent us pictures, and of course Franz was beautiful."

Joe and Billie made arrangements to have Franz brought over from Germany. But in the process of being gelded, Franz almost died.

"We didn't know if Franz was going to make it or not," says Billie. "We already had pictures of him and felt like we were adopting a child. This beautiful picture of him became a cornerstone in our house, and we would cover it in daisies

like a little shrine. We were so worried about Franz. It took nine months of medical care before he was fit to travel. One of the problems was that at seven he was probably too old to geld. He didn't respond well to the anesthesia. Anyway, after that Joe and I made up our minds that we were never going to sell our horses. Orien and Franz are part of the family, and they are staying with us until they go peacefully into the night."

"Franz is such an amazing horse," says Joe. "He's more than sixteen hands high, which is big for a Friesian. His mane goes all the way from the top of his ears down his back to way past his knee bone. He has a huge and very thick forelock, and if all that hair was unbraided it would be impossible to see his face."

"Orien is a little leaner and smaller, with a beautiful face and sweet personality," adds Billie. "He is much spunkier to ride than Franz, who is more calm and easygoing. When the two of them walk out, Franz is definitely the showstopper, but Joe and I love them both dearly."

"To see a Friesian is to love it," enthuses Joe. "Just being around Orien and Franz is therapeutic. I like coming down the driveway and seeing them greet me. They are artistically beautiful. To us, there are Friesians and then there are all the other horses!"

For her part, Billie appreciates how having horses has brought her family closer together. "Our boys ride, and they are emotionally tied to our horses. Roman and I will go up to the barn, and he will take out the miniature horse that we have and brush him while I groom Orien. For Joe and I, being with the horses is something that we both love and enjoy together, and this bonding makes our relationship that much more special."

KATHARINE ROSS AND CLEO ELLIOTT

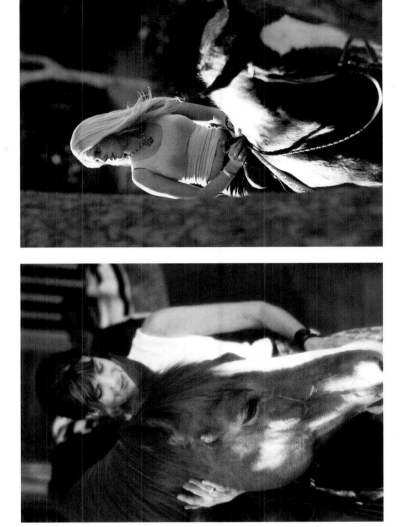

Like Mother, Like Daughter

KATHARINE ROSS HAS THE DISTINCTION OF COSTARRING WITH DUSTIN HOFFMAN, ROBERT REDFORD, AND PAUL NEWMAN IN TWO OF THE MOST CRITICALLY ACCLAIMED FILMS OF ALL TIME: *The Graduate*, FOR WHICH SHE RECEIVED AN ACADEMY AWARD NOMINATION, AND *Butch Cassidy and the Sundance Kid.* THE CHARACTERS OF ELAINE ROBINSON AND ETTA PLACE HAVE BEEN EMBEDDED IN THE CONSCIOUSNESS OF BABY BOOMERS AS WELL AS THEIR CHILDREN, WHO HAVE SEEN THESE GREAT AND ENDURING FILMS ON THE SMALL SCREEN.

HOWEVER, ROSS'S OFF-SCREEN LIFE IS PERHAPS EVEN MORE REWARDING THAN HER MOVIE CAREER. SHE LIVES IN NORTHERN MALIBU, CALIFORNIA, WITH HER HUSBAND, RENOWNED ACTOR SAM ELLIOTT, AND THEIR NINETEEN-YEAR-OLD DAUGHTER, CLEO, ON A REMARKABLE TWO-AND-A-HALF-ACRE *ranchito* THAT BOASTS A POND AND TRICKLING STREAM THAT WINDS ITS WAY DOWN TO THE PACIFIC OCEAN. ROSS FOUND THIS PARCEL OF LAND, WHICH HAPPENED TO BE OWNED BY *Gunsmoke* STAR JAMES ARNESS, IN 1975. ROSS'S HORSES SHARE THE PROPERTY, WHICH INCLUDES A SMALL BARN, A WORKING ROUND PEN, A HERD OF CATS AND DOGS, AND AN EXTRAORDINARY GARDEN.

ROSS'S DEEP LOVE OF ANIMALS IN GENERAL AND HORSES IN PARTICULAR, WHICH SHE'S PASSED ON TO CLEO, HAS RESULTED IN A WONDERFUL AND ONGOING MOTHER-DAUGHTER BOND.

"I've had horses in my backyard

for twenty years," says Katharine. "I used to ride every day, early in the morning, from our backyard down to the water. But of course things have changed dramatically over the last two decades in Malibu. The area has been developed. The tide pools are constantly evolving, and damaging erosion has hit the beaches. I still love riding early in the morning, but it is now a much greater commitment of time, as I have to hitch up Ms. Kitty and North and trailer them into the foothills of the Santa Monica Mountains fifteen to twenty minutes away. The almost daily casual rides that I loved so much now take a three-hour block of time, but I still try to go out at least twice a week, depending on my schedule.

"Sometimes I ride with my daughter, Cleo, and at other times with my friend Patty, who is actually responsible for Wesley, a third horse that is now in my life. Horses seem to gravitate to me, and Ms. Kitty is the only horse that I have actually bought. Wesley belonged to the father of a friend of Patty's who died of pancreatic cancer. The family didn't know what to do with Wesley, and so they asked me to take care of him. I agreed, but on the condition that Patty would help me care for him as well.

"Patty and I ride Ms. Kitty and Wesley and we free-lead North through the trails and across the fields. North is another horse I inherited. Well into his twenties, he is semi-retired, but I can't imagine going riding without him. He is so good that we simply tie a lead rope around his neck, let him be a free horse, and when we call or whistle, dear North comes back to us.

"North is truly *The Man Who Came to Dinner*—he came for

a short stay after I volunteered to help out another friend who was going through a divorce and could not afford his upkeep. He's the reason our motto at this house is, "Once you come through the gate, you don't leave until you go feet first." North is living proof of that. Who knows how old he is, but he's obviously got some warmblood in him, and he's our North!"

Katharine stops for a moment, allowing her memories to carry her back in time, and then continues, "I remember falling in love with horses at the age of seven when on my first pony ride. It was just riding around in circles, and I was jumping around very uncomfortably on these rough-gaited little animals, but I was grinning from ear to ear just the same. I was hooked the first time I rode and always wanted my own horse. When I was a young girl, my family knew this couple who owned two giant Tennessee Walkers more than seventeen hands high, and I would ride up in front on their saddles.

"My own horse was the first thing that I bought after I did my first movie, *Shenandoah*. He was only eight months old and way to young to ride, but I bought him just the same and ultimately pastured him for two years until he matured. In my ignorance I trained him myself, and he was never more than green broke, but I rode him for more than thirty years."

She pauses again, remembering how daughter Cleo came into the world. "Riding has always taken me away from my problems. I always come back feeling much better than when I started out. I rode my two earlier horses, Johnny and Joker, every day when I was pregnant with Cleo. Finally when I was about eight months pregnant I could not get on my horse, as there was too much in front of me. One day I was riding and the next day I was too big. The first time I took Cleo riding

she was seven weeks old, and four years later I gave her Joker."

At this point, Cleo takes up the story.

"I have been riding my whole life, as Mom took me riding on Johnny when I was just seven weeks old. As a little girl I would go into their stalls and just sit on their backs. I never really played with dolls growing up, as I was much more interested in Breyer model horses. Not having any brothers or sisters, horses became my playmates. I even got a horse tattoo. I was born loving these animals, and they're still a huge part of my life. This is something that my mother and I share.

Katharine is happy to agree. "I enjoy riding with her so much. It is important to share this wonderful experience with her—both the love for horses and the pleasure of riding them. This is a connection that we will always have."

"The perfect ride for me," says Cleo, "is being on horse that I feel very connected to, surrounded by beautiful scenery. I've always had a comfortable relationship with horses, just like my mom has. She passed this natural ability on to me. We both like being around them, and they in turn feel comfortable around us as well. Hopefully as I grow up I will be in a financial position to have horses on my own property, as I would love to have as many of these wonderful beings as I can afford."

"I really do see some of myself in Cleo," observes Katharine. "When a woman has a daughter, it is wonderful to share with her things that you love and give you pleasure."

Cleo, it is clear, accepts this motherly gift in the spirit in which it was given. "It is hard to put into words what makes this relationship with horses and my mom so special. Horses are more than mere animals; they are also our friends, and if you both respect and take care of them, they will love you back."

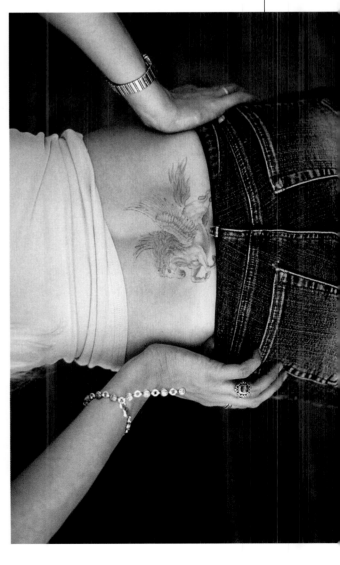

JANE SEYMOUR

A Hand for Driving

MULTIPLE EMMY AWARD– AND GOLDEN GLOBE–WINNING ACTRESS JANE SEYMOUR HAS STARRED IN SOME OF TELEVISION'S MOST MEMORABLE MINISERIES, INCLUDING *East of Eden*, *War and Remembrance*, AND *Onassis*, IN WHICH SHE PLAYED MARIA CALLAS. SEYMOUR IS, HOWEVER, PERHAPS BEST KNOWN FOR HER STARRING ROLE IN THE LONG-RUNNING TELEVISION SERIES *Dr. Quinn, Medicine Woman*, IN WHICH SHE GOT TO SHOW OFF HER SKILL WITH HORSES. BORN AND RAISED IN ENGLAND, SEYMOUR'S EARLY TRAINING WAS IN BALLET, THOUSANDS OF MILES AND MANY CAREERS AWAY FROM THE FRONTIER WORLD OF HEARTY PIONEER DOCTOR MICHAELA QUINN.

TODAY, SEYMOUR CONTINUES TO WORK WITH HORSES. IN 2003 SHE STARRED IN *Touching Wild Horses*, A HEARTWARMING DRAMA ABOUT A YOUNG MAN WHO IS SENT TO LIVE WITH HIS RECLUSIVE AUNT FIONA (PLAYED BY SEYMOUR) ON A REMOTE ISLAND, WHERE THE TWO FORM A BOND WITH A HERD OF WILD HORSES. IN REAL LIFE, ALL FOUR OF SEYMOUR'S CHILDREN RIDE, AND HER HUSBAND, ACTOR JAMES KEACH, WAS ONE OF THE WRITERS, PRODUCERS, AND STARS OF THE CONTEMPORARY WESTERN CLASSIC *The Long Riders*. A TRUE RENAISSANCE WOMAN, SEYMOUR IS ALSO THE WRITER OF THE ACCLAIMED CHILDREN'S SERIES *This One and That One*, AND HER ARTWORK HAS BEEN FEATURED IN ONE-WOMAN SHOWS ACROSS THE COUNTRY.

WE CAUGHT UP WITH SEYMOUR AT THE BONY PONY RANCH IN THE MALIBU MOUNTAINS, WHERE SHE DROVE HER HORSE AND WAGON FROM *Dr. Quinn* ONE MORE TIME.

Over the last twenty-plus years, horses

have been very important to me both on and off the screen. It all goes back to *The Four Feathers*, which I starred in with Beau Bridges. I fell in love with the discipline of riding sidesaddle in that film. Growing up as a ballerina, I felt very comfortable turning my spine toward the direction the horse was moving while leaving my legs on the left-hand side. I balanced myself by crossing my legs around the pommel, which is like a saddle horn. Riding in this position made me feel very safe; if the horse reared around, I was firmly attached to the middle of the saddle and wasn't sliding off of the front or the back. I could canter and gallop in full period costume. I have often thought that if I had continued riding in a serious way, the sidesaddle would have been my choice.

Years later I starred in the remake of the Daphne Du Maurier thriller *Jamaica Inn* and fell in love with this wonderful horse named James. In the movie he was ridden by another actor, but at the end of project I bought both him and the castle in England where we were filming. James was really a film horse when we got him, but soon that steed became a member of our family.

Even though I have ridden in many movies, more often than not I have driven horses, and I am actually very good at it. I've driven four-in-hand and actually attempted six-in-hand once, which was pretty impossible given the size of my hands. On *Dr. Quinn, Medicine Woman*, almost every day of shooting I'd be on that wagon. Driving horses is, to me, like riding a

horse except that you are not sitting on the animal. This is a very delicate thing, to persuade them to move in a particular way by giving cues to their mouths. You have to be pretty strong to have full control, as well as a good horse and light touch to finesse their double bridles. The wranglers on the show always liked working with me, as I had a gentle touch with the horses. And I think the horses liked me as well; they were usually well behaved, and we never had a serious mishap.

It was interesting that the producers never even asked me if I knew how to ride a horse before they cast me in the starring role. In that first week I had to canter and be accosted by Indians on a tiny path where all the horses were rearing and charging around me. I thought it was very amusing. When the right mo-

"YOU HAVE TO BE PRETTY STRONG TO HAVE FULL CONTROL, AS WELL AS A GOOD HORSE AND LIGHT TOUCH TO FINESSE THEIR DOUBLE BRIDLES."

ment came along, I told the producers and wranglers that they were very lucky because I did know how to ride. From then on the cowboys let me do most of my own driving on the show.

Film riding is very different from regular riding. You can't go gently from a walk to a trot to a canter but have to charge out from behind a tree at full gallop, stop on a dime at your mark, and then recite a few pages of dialogue. I became good at that kind of precision driving and could land my horses and buggy on exactly the right spot. Then there were other times on *Dr. Quinn* that I had the wagon and horses going at a full

canter. Once I had to drive Jane Wyman at full speed and she really freaked out! But I felt so comfortable that I even drove when I was seven months pregnant with my twin boys.

Before *Dr. Quinn*, I drove horses in *Somewhere in Time* with Christopher Reeve. In that film I played an actress, and there is a scene where I run away from my manager to spend the day with Chris, who is a playwright. I was wearing an Edwardian gown that was beautiful and elegant but very constricting, and we jumped into a carriage and went off around Mackinac Island in Michigan, which was where we were

shooting. In fact, we had to ride everywhere in a buggy because no cars were allowed on the island. The Teamsters had to drive the horses to take the actors to the set. The film had a wonderful leisurely pace about it, as the crew could only go as fast or slow as the horses could carry the equipment from one location to the next.

Perhaps driving horses is more of a British sport these days. I remember many years ago when I interviewed Prince Philip on *Good Morning America* about the upcoming marriage of Prince Andrew and Sarah Ferguson, Philip gave me the royal scoop about the horses that were going to pull the wedding carriage. It gave me great pride to see the streets lined with hundreds of thousands of spectators waiting for these remarkable horses and an elegant carriage to come prancing down the wedding route and up to the church—and to realize that I drove horses too!

MARIA SHRIVER

The Reward of Accomplishment

MARIA SHRIVER IS ACCOMPLISHED IN SO MANY AREAS OF HER LIFE. SHE'S A WIFE AND THE MOTHER OF FOUR CHILDREN. SHE'S AN NBC NEWS CORRESPONDENT AND A CONTRIBUTING ANCHOR FOR *Dateline NBC* WHO HAS WON NUMEROUS AWARDS, INCLUDING AN EMMY AND TWO PEABODY FOR HER JOURNALISM. AND SHE'S A BESTSELLING AUTHOR. HER FIRST BOOK, A CHILDREN'S STORY FILLED WITH QUESTIONS AND ANSWERS ABOUT DEATH AND CALLED *What's Heaven?* HAS SOLD CLOSE TO A MILLION COPIES. *Ten Things I Wish I'd Known Before I Went Out into the Real World* CHRONICLES HER LIFE AND CAREER. IN HER THIRD BESTSELLER SHE HELPS YOUNG PEOPLE UNDERSTAND THOSE WHO HAVE DISABILITIES IN *What's Wrong with Timmy?* CONTINUING TO WRITE ABOUT IMPORTANT, COMPLEX AND TOPICAL ISSUES, IN 2004 SHRIVER RELEASED *What's Happening to Grandpa?* WHICH DEALS WITH THE ISSUE OF ALZHEIMER'S DISEASE.

SHRIVER GREW UP SITTING ASTRIDE HER BELOVED PONY MISS BUCK, AND SHE STILL RIDES FOR PLEASURE. JUST AS SHE COMPETED IN REGIONAL HORSE SHOWS AS A YOUNG GIRL, HER FOURTEEN-YEAR-OLD DAUGHTER, KATHERINE, NOW CARRIES THE TORCH. STILL MOURNING THE PASSING OF HER THOROUGHBRED, RECKLESS PASSION, SHRIVER AND HER HUSBAND, GOVERNOR ARNOLD SCHWARZENEGGER OF CALIFORNIA, BOTH RIDE ARNOLD'S BEAUTIFUL WHITE ANDALUSIAN, CAMPY.

MARIA SHRIVER JUMPING AT THE AGE OF EIGHT

Riding for me was first a way to escape

all the male energy in my house. I was the only girl in a family with four brothers and a lot of male cousins. If my brothers each had several friends over, there would be me and about twenty boys throwing basketballs and footballs at my head. I came from a very sports-oriented family, and so I really needed to find something that I did that was all my own. Riding gave me a sense of identity and a sense of accomplishment. It was also a very nurturing experience because I took care of my horse.

Riding was also very competitive and nurtured this aspect of my life. My family was competitive, and maybe that helped me to excel in the sport. Unlike a team sport, competitive riding is independent, and it fulfilled a lot of things for me that I may not have even been conscious of at the time.

When I was in school, girls were not participating in a lot of sports and there was no Title 9 (mandated co-ed sports funding) program. Even though I was very athletic, most of the girls I knew were not on sports teams. Luckily, I started riding at the age of three or four. When I look back at pictures of me as a little girl, I was frequently sitting on a horse, so either my mother or father must have put me there. My grandfather had a stable in Massachusetts and I rode there in the summer with him when I was really little. I started to ride competitively when I was about seven or eight and had this little buckskin pony named Miss Buck. She was only about twelve hands high, but I ended up spending most of my childhood on that pony. Miss Buck and I went through all kinds of local schooling

"I HAVE NEVER HAD A RELATIONSHIP WITH ANOTHER ANIMAL THAT HAD THE SAME INTENSITY OF EMOTION."

shows and moved up to the "A" shows and then to the indoor shows as well as summer shows. Riding was really my identity.

At the end of sixth grade, when my dad became the Ambassador to France, my family moved there, and we took Miss Buck with us. I didn't show her in France, but I still loved riding her there just the same. She lived in Europe with us for two years, and when we came home, Miss Buck came with us. I basically outgrew her at fifteen, but I decided to keep and breed her on our farm. She was my friend—I have never had a relationship with another animal that had the same intensity of emotion.

Riding is now something that I encourage my kids to do, especially the girls, who both ride. During my competition years, I never could understand why my mother was always so nervous when I rode and was jumping. I loved to jump and to jump high. Now when my oldest daughter, Katherine, jumps, I understand. It's so nerve wracking. But Arnold and I do go to shows with her.

Last summer the family went to a dude ranch in Colorado because I thought it would be fun to do some Western riding. My boys were like, "Ugh," while my daughters and I had such a great time riding and rounding up cattle together. You see so few boys

riding at horse shows, and more girls than you can shake a stick at. If I were a boy I would be on a horse so fast, but they just don't seem to have the same bond.

Anytime I ride it creates a sense of freedom and a feeling of accomplishment. I love cantering along, being on a beautiful animal with my hair blowing behind me. Sadly, my horse recently passed away, so now when I can, I ride Arnold's big and beautiful white Andalusian.

Looking back, riding gave me a sense of self at the age when young girls need to feel accomplished. Katherine is on the equestrian team at school, and I can see that it gives her a sense of confidence. As girls handle such a powerful animal, and handle it well, it gives them a sense of their own strength and capabilities. It is such an important thing for children to have something that they really love and can say, "I am something!" Katherine can say, "I am a champion horse rider," and even if she never competes again, she will have achieved that. She can look back and tell her own children, "Look at my blue ribbons hanging on my wall," and "Look at all my silver trays with my name on them," and I think that is a really important thing.

MARIA WITH HUSBAND GOV. SCHWARZENEGGER'S BEAUTIFUL WHITE ANDALUSIAN, CAMPY

ROBERT WAGNER
AND JILL ST. JOHN

Our Cowboy Life

A May-to-December friendship with Clark Gable launched Robert Wagner's film career and created a deep love for the film legend's horse, Steele. Growing up in elite Bel Air, California, Wagner met Gable at the local country club where the young man worked as a caddy. A walk-on role led to a small part in *The Halls of Montezuma* with Jack Palance and featured roles in *Titanic*, *A Kiss Before Dying*, *The True Story of Jesse James*, and *The Longest Day* opposite Sean Connery and Richard Burton. Yet in spite of his early film success, Wagner really came into his own on the little screen with such television hits as *It Takes a Thief*, *Switch*, and *Hart to Hart*. He became cool to a whole new generation of 1990s moviegoers with his costarring roles in the phenomenally successful *Austin Powers: International Man of Mystery* and *Austin Powers: The Spy Who Shagged Me.*

Most recently, Wagner has starred in *Play It to the Bone* with Antonio Banderas, in the E! Entertainment original movie *Becoming Dick*, and in *Rocket's Red Glare* for the Fox Family Channel.

And what man between the age of forty-five and ninety can forget the beautiful redhead in the bikini who costarred in the 1971 James Bond film *Diamonds are For-

ever*? Her name is Jill St. John and she started wowing audiences at the age of five. She has also appeared in such films as *Come Blow Your Horn* and *Tony Rome*. An accomplished culinary expert, St. John has been the in-house cooking expert on *Good Morning America* and food columnist for *USA Weekend*.

St. John's passion turned from culinary to equine when she married Wagner in 1990. Since then, the two have shared a remarkable fifteen years with their beloved horses. Living in the urban yet surprisingly private com-

munity of Brentwood, just blocks away from busy Los Angeles streets, St. John and Wagner pride themselves on being horse people. Wagner loves looking out of their kitchen window and seeing his favorite horse, Sloan, just twenty feet away from him, and St. John looks forward to her early morning rides up into the Santa Monica Mountains with saddlebags packed with carrots for her horse Dexter and iced cappuccino for her.

"I am a cowgirl and RJ is a cowboy,"

says Jill St. John plainly about her and her husband, Robert Wagner. "We don't have elegant riding habits and beautiful boots. I get on my Western saddle, wearing a plaid shirt, chaps, and Argentine hat, because I don't like a traditional cowboy hat on me, and I'm off on my little Western horse. We live with our horses and are very lucky to have them at home, which is very unusual in Los Angeles."

"We also had a working and very professional ranch where we bred and raised Quarter Horses," adds Robert. "The ranch boasted a six-time champion Quarter Horse stallion that is now gone, and I really got into the business aspect of horses and loved it. We started off in the Thoroughbred racing business for a while, which was a whole different part of our life with horses. Then we started to raise Arabian horses with my daughter, but soon became very interested in the cutting horse business. Cutting horses are remarkable. A well-trained one will perform so beautifully that you just sit there and marvel."

For her part, Jill revels in her everyday involvement with her horses, and she points out how they touch every aspect of her life with Robert. "My husband has a world champion

mare and my personal horse is a Pacific Coast champion. They are both Quarter Horses from the DocBar line, the ones that won all the money. At our house in Aspen we have a display area with horse pictures and paintings and there is a picture of little six-year-old RJ on a horse!"

"I was absolutely engaged with horses at such a young age," admits Robert. "My father always rode horses and had a place in northern Michigan where I would go to camp and where I started riding ponies. When my father moved to California, he bought some other horses and I was totally involved with them growing up. I actually showed horses across the street from where I lived. We lived near the Bel Air Hotel in Los Angeles, and when World War II broke out, all the groomsmen who worked at the hotel stables went into the service, so I helped take care of those horses at the age of twelve or thirteen. Three of us young boys were called into stable action, including the late John Derek.

"My father also had a trick horse named Sonny that he got from this fellow in Arizona, and he would do absolutely everything I would show him once in a while. Sonny would lie down

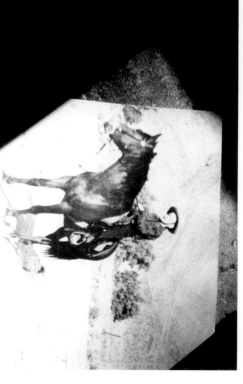

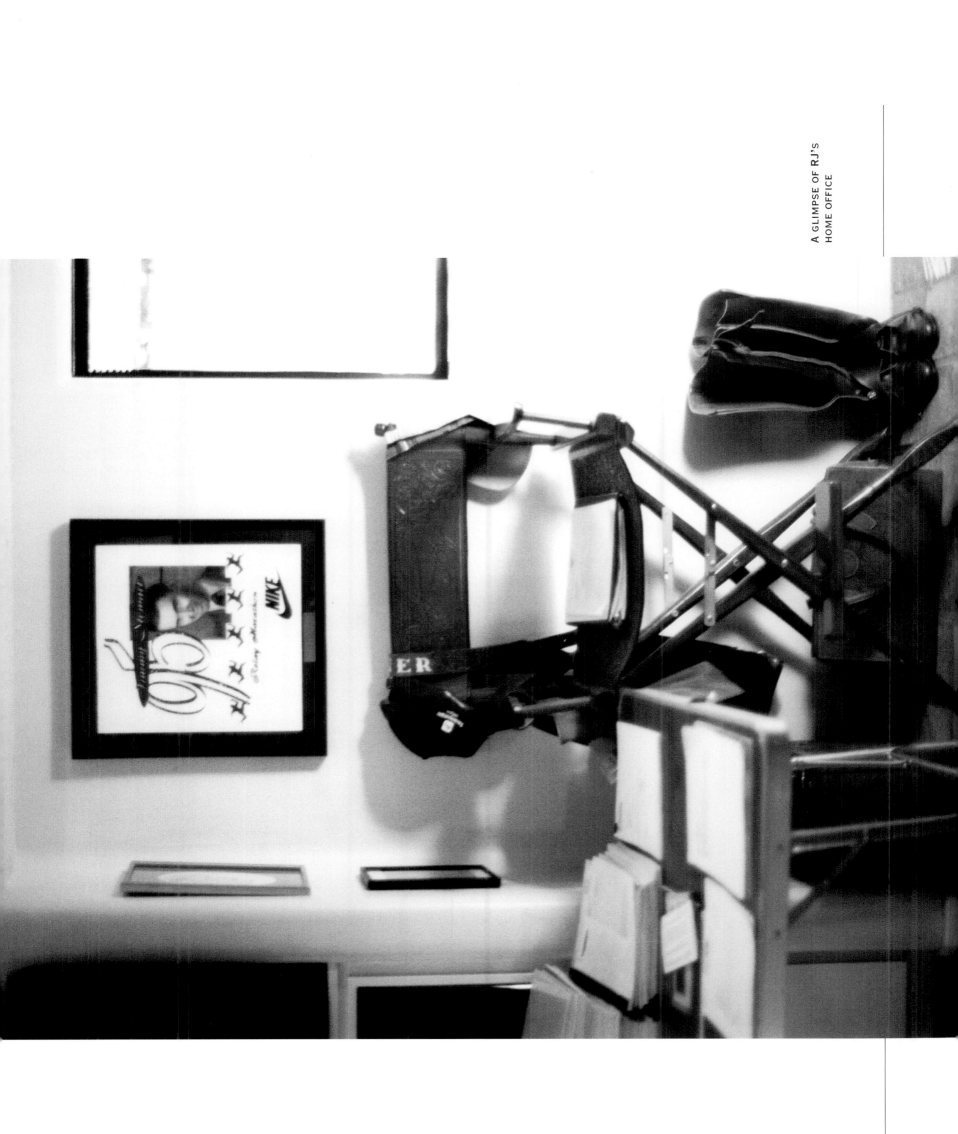

and I would crawl over and get on his back and he'd get up and carry me out of the ring. He would also bow and even shake his head yes and no. Sonny had one big white spot on his shoulder with a flaxen mane and tail. He was a great, great horse, and when he was too old to be ridden any more, my father and I took him back to Arizona and turned him loose on the ranch of the man we bought him from, and that is where he died. I still have a picture of my dad on him.

"There were several years when I was living in Europe that horses were not prominent in my life, but my daughter Katie brought me right back into it. We bought the house that Jill and I are living in now and have four horses living with us that are almost in petting distance. Starting out as an actor, I would drive by here and say, 'If only I could have a house like this in my life . . .' We have chickens, doves, and dogs, as well as our horses, here. They all mean a great deal to us.

"Jill and I consider ourselves real horse people because we don't hand the reins over to someone else to do the work. We take care of our own horses; we feed them, wash them, and clean out their feet."

Jill adds, "We even have a foaling barn, and several horses have been born right here. In fact, the last horse born here is still on our property. They are so affectionate and so social. You build such a bond. We've gotten to know them and they've gotten to know us. I'll walk out into the barn and Dexter actually starts to drool. He knows that I am going to give him a carrot or a horse cookie."

"It's sort of like me, you know. I sort of drool too when I see you walking! But Jill has a different story in her life with horses, which is quite a good one."

"I've always loved horses but I was afraid of them for a long time. I would touch them, and if they moved I would get scared. As a very young woman I had several bad experiences with horses, including being thrown and falling off several times. When I met RJ, I saw how much

> **"I WAS ABSOLUTELY ENGAGED WITH HORSES AT A VERY YOUNG AGE."**

he loved these animals, and I got tired of being afraid of them. So I went and got hypnotized, and after one session the hypnotist said, 'What are you afraid of?' and I said, 'Falling off.' She worked on my fear and now I ride every day."

In addition to having their own animals right on their property, this horse-loving couple live just a block and a half away from a wonderful ten-acre riding facility and also close to riding trails that

lead up into the Santa Monica Mountains. "If I wanted to ride for three full days, I could end up at the ocean and ride on the beach," says Jill. "I love riding in the early morning and packing my saddlebags with treats for me and Dexter. Several friends and I take this wonderful four-hour ride and go through little streams where there are wildflowers, butterflies, and birds that make you so grateful to be alive."

Jill tells the story of how she came to know Dexter, now her favorite horse. "RJ kept giving me these horses and I would ride them but there would be no chemistry. He would bring them in from the ranch that we owned in Hidden Valley, and I would ride each one for a week and say, 'No, I don't think so,' and he would send it back and another one would arrive. So, I am out at the ranch one day and get on a horse named Dexter. I tell RJ that this is the horse for me. He says, 'You can't have him. I have given you my best horses and you keep sending them back, so you can't have Dexter.' Well, not long after this, one day I am riding a three-year-old Thoroughbred with my instructor and the next thing I know we are both on the ground. The horse I was riding had died of a cerebral hemorrhage and I broke my back. RJ brings me back from the hospital, is very solicitous, and helps me into bed. I look up at him and say, 'Now can I have Dexter?' So Dexter is mine now, and has been mine for twelve years. He's got the smoothest gait; I always say that riding Dexter is like riding a sofa. But he also has a lot of fire and eats too much, so I am constantly putting him on a diet. One day I am out at the ring and a little girl is screaming bloody murder, so I come over and she says, 'Dexter ate my Chicken McNuggets!' He is such fun, and I swear he has a permanent smile on his face."

Speaking of smiles and good times, both of these fun-loving souls feel that owning horses has brought them closer together. Consider how they describe their ranch in Hidden Valley, forty-five miles outside of Los Angeles.

"There was nothing on the property—we created and built everything that is there," explains Jill. "We used to go to the ranch on the weekends and have dinner in this little two-room apartment. Just imagine two stalls made into an apartment. We just loved it."

"I think those years were some of the greatest we've ever had," adds Robert. "It was so romantic and such fun to know that we were the ones who had made the choice of putting this mare with that stallion. That ranch was just magical. We had these ATV motorcycles and after dinner we would get on them with a big bag of carrots on the back and go out into the moonlight and feed the horses. This was a real dream for Jill and me, and it will always be something that we have in our hearts."

"JILL AND I CONSIDER OURSELVES REAL HORSE PEOPLE BECAUSE WE DON'T HAND THE REINS OVER TO SOMEONE ELSE TO DO THE WORK."

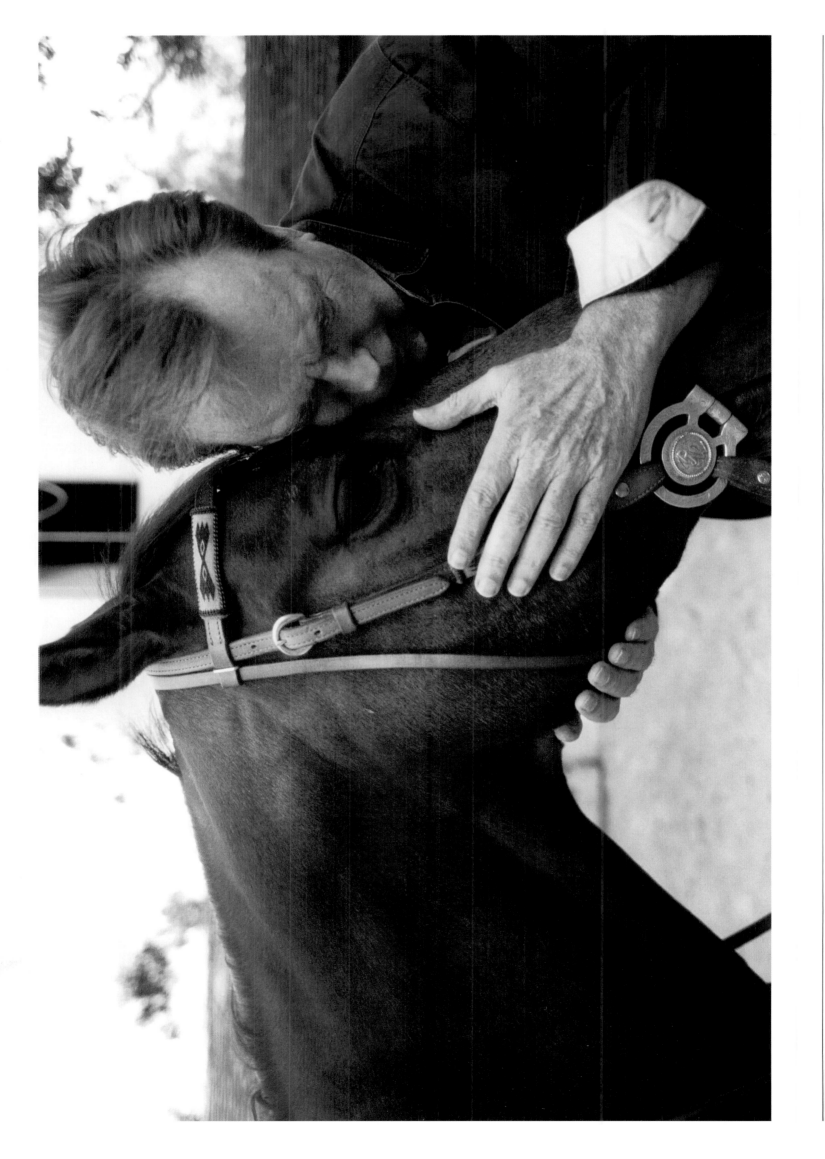

JEFF BRIDGES

A History with Horses

Jeff Bridges has been lighting up the big screen ever since 1972 when he earned a Best Supporting Oscar nomination for his standout work in *The Last Picture Show*. In that remarkable, award-winning film, Bridges costarred as a high school football hero coming of age in a small Texas town during the 1950s. Since then he has proven his unique talent for challenging, character-driven roles, as in John Huston's *Fat City*, *Thunderbolt and Lightfoot*, where he received another Best Supporting Actor nod, *Star Man*, *Jagged Edge*, *The Fisher King*, and *The Big Lebowski*, among many other memorable performances.

Such talent definitely runs in the family. Jeff's father, Lloyd Bridges, spurred a scuba-diving

craze in the late 1950s with his starring role in the ultra cool television series *Sea Hunt*, and his work in Westerns, including the classic *High Noon*, instilled in Jeff a love of horses. Brother Beau, also an actor, costarred with Jeff in *The Fabulous Baker Boys* in 1989.

We caught up with the four-time Academy Award nominee on the set of the big 2003 summer movie *Seabiscuit*, which received both Golden Globe and Academy Award nominations for Best Picture, where he starred as Charles Howard, the visionary owner of a down-and-out horse that galloped into the hearts of millions during the Great Depression. It was a role that came naturally to Bridges.

The improbable success of *Seabiscuit*

makes for a great story, and my history with the project is an interesting one. My cousin, Kathy Simpson, called me several years ago and had just read the book *Seabiscuit* and told me that I had to play the role of Charles Howard. I said, "Yeah, maybe one day I'll read the book." Years passed, and then one day this script came down the pipe, and I realized it was the wonderful story that Kathy had been talking about. So I called my agent.

Seabiscuit is a classic underdog story. Charles Howard was the largest Buick dealer west of the Mississippi during the 1930s when he decided he wanted to get out of the automo-

bile business, and, in spite of advice against it, he purchased a horse called Seabiscuit. Everyone thought the horse was a loser, even though he came from Man o' War stock. He had a terrible track record, and they believed Howard was crazy for buying him. But with the help of the trainer, played by Chris Cooper in the movie, and the jockey, played by Tobey Maguire, that horse became a champion, as well as a hero.

It is so wonderful to have it received the way that it has been, and it is especially gratifying to have people that enjoyed the book so much enjoy the movie as well. All the heart that is in the book is also in the movie. Author Laura Hillenbrand helped me out a lot when I was trying to make Howard my own by lending me photographs of him, and she also lent me a wallet of his that I carried around every day—it was sort of a touchstone piece.

Perhaps part of my attraction to Charles Howard and to the movie stemmed from my lifelong love of horses and the fact that I grew up around them. My dad, Lloyd, loved to ride, and whenever he was in a Western he would frequently come home dressed as a cowboy. I would dress up in his cowboy costumes and try on the boots and hat and run around the house like that. He loved making Westerns, and the riding part was always his favorite. Dad was a wonderful horseman and taught all of his kids how to ride at an early age. *High Noon* was the most famous Western that he was involved with, but I also loved *The Tall Texan* and *Little Big Horn*, two really good but lesser known films.

I was a real horseracing fan, too; I would go to the track with my grandfather, who bet on Seabiscuit before I was born.

These days I spend as much time as I can with my own horses at our ranch in Montana. I really love it up there—it's

"I WOULD GO TO THE TRACK WITH MY GRANDFATHER, WHO BET ON SEABISCUIT BEFORE I WAS BORN."

a wonderful riding environment. The ranch is up against national forest, so there are thousands of acres behind our house where we can go riding. They call it the Big Sky Country and the sky does seems bigger in Montana, where the weather is constantly changing. It is wonderful to go riding there and to be part of the landscape and even get lost out in the wilderness and enjoy the streams, forest, sky, and mountains. It is nice to be alone, but it is also great to share the experience with someone else. My father used to love that, and we would ride together in Montana on a regular basis.

It is also so remarkable what you can learn from horses. I remember going to a Ray Hunt clinic in Montana where he was green breaking horses, and so much he had to say about them related to raising my daughters. Ray was saying how important it was to handle the horses feet, but at the same time you should never let them know that they're stronger than you. If the horse pulls away you need to let them know that you intended for him to pull away. And the same thing is true for kids. In my relationship with my kids, because I love them so much, it can be tough to stick to my guns in a discipline situation. Horses are so much stronger than you, so you can't out muscle them, you just have to set boundaries and make the relationship work.

CHRISTIE BRINKLEY

A Cut Above

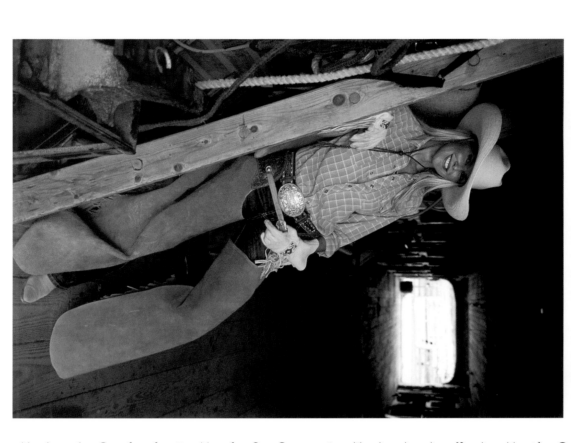

CHRISTIE BRINKLEY HAS EPITOMIZED ALL-AMERICAN BEAUTY FOR THREE DECADES, AND SHE SHOWS NO SIGNS OF SLOWING DOWN. SHE HAS APPEARED ON MORE THAN SIX HUNDRED MAGAZINE COVERS AROUND THE WORLD AND WAS THE FIRST MODEL TO HAVE THREE CONSECUTIVE *Sports Illustrated* BATHING SUIT ISSUE COVERS IN A ROW—AND SHE IS THE ONLY ONE TO HAVE BEEN FEATURED EXCLUSIVELY IN ALL TWELVE MONTHS OF THE BEST-SELLING CALENDAR. BRINKLEY HAS ALSO PRODUCED FOUR OF HER OWN BEST-SELLING CALENDARS AND POSTERS, AS WELL AS AUTHORED *Christie Brinkley's Outdoor Beauty & Fitness Guide,* WHICH MADE THE *New York Times* BESTSELLER LIST.

IN ADDITION, BRINKLEY WAS THE SPOKESWOMAN FOR COVER GIRL FOR A REMARKABLE TWENTY YEARS, THE LONGEST-RUNNING COSMETICS CONTRACT EVER. SHE HAS BEEN A FREQUENT GUEST ON TALK SHOWS, GUEST-STARRED ON NBC'S *Mad About You,* AND EVEN HOSTED HER OWN DAILY SHOW, *Living in the 90s with Christie Brinkley.* IN 2003, VH1 NAMED BRINKLEY ONE OF THE TOP 200 POP CULTURE ICONS OF ALL TIME. SHE WAS THE "GIRL IN THE RED FERRARI" IN THE NATIONAL LAMPOON VACATION MOVIES. OTHERS MAY CALL HER THE "UPTOWN GIRL" FROM THE BILLY JOEL VIDEOS, BUT BRINKLEY DESCRIBES HERSELF AS "A MOTHER, ARTIST, AND ENVIRONMENTAL ACTIVIST" WHOSE GREATEST JOY IS SHARING NATURE'S BEAUTY WITH HER FAMILY: HUSBAND PETER COOK, AN ARCHITECT; DAUGHTER ALEXA, 18, WHO IS A MUSICIAN; SON JACK, 8½, AND DAUGHTER SAILOR, 5½, WHO ARE BOTH ARTISTS.

(WE CAUGHT UP WITH BRINKLEY AT DIANE AND RUSTY LEAVER'S DEEP HOLLOW RANCH IN MONTAUK, NEW YORK, THE OLDEST CATTLE RANCH IN THE WORLD).

I was one of those typical little girls

who just loved horses and would dream about riding them all the time. My family would go out to Palm Springs when it was still a desert, and we would stay at a dude ranch where they let my brother and me work in the stables. They allowed us to muck the stalls, soap the saddles, and brush the horses. It was a lot of work, but we loved it because we thought it was such a privilege just to be around the horses. Once the chores were done, we would get to ride the horses across the desert. It was so much fun!

However, whenever I did get the chance to ride, I was always getting bucked off or thrown. I would picture myself galloping across the range like they did in Westerns, but in reality it was my horse that the tumbleweed was always blowing in front of! I would always get the old nag that would take off and turn back in the direction of the barn. I was so afraid before a ride that my teeth would actually ache. But nothing could deter me from getting back in the saddle. I was determined to sit it right.

This is how it went with horses and me, until I finally got my very own horse from Billy. I woke up one Christmas morning and there was a white horse out on the lawn wearing a big red ribbon. That horse, Belle Star, was a retired polo pony, and we got to know and trust each other so intimately. My fears became a thing of the past, and I was finally able to really enjoy a ride without a trip to the orthopedist. I took care of my horse and my horse took care of me.

When we moved out to the Hamptons, I rode English-style just like every one else out here, but I realized that I really didn't want to ride in circles around in the ring, so I sat a Western saddle and moved Belle to Montauk, where there is the oldest ranch in America. Deep Hollow is a four-thou-sand-acre cattle ranch with ponds and beaches, so I could ful-fill my fantasy of galloping across the wide-open spaces.

One day I was flipping through the television channels at home and saw this incredible horse leaping back and forth doing these really wild moves. The rider looked like he was doing nothing more than going along for the ride. The next day when I was out riding in Montauk, I mentioned what I had seen to several people and they told me it was a cutting horse. They said they used to train cutting horses out on Long Island a long time ago.

Well, to me it looked like a lot of fun. So I ordered a *Learn to Cut* video that they were promoting on ESPN, along with a fake cow, which is a kite strung across a corral and op-erated by bicycle pedals. Some pals and I watched the video-tape, hooked up the fake cow, and started to get our horses to follow us. Then we rented a real herd of cattle, and it soon became apparent that we needed to get some authentic cut-ting horses from Texas. Working with those horses was such a blast that we decided to rent some real cattle and bring them to the Deep Hollow Ranch in Montauk. The Deep Hollow Ranch is steeped in Western tradition, so we would have rodeos and do barrel racing and egg-and-spoon relays.

We even did a Flag Beaning Quadrille, and all the while we kept practicing our cutting.

It was then that we decided to produce a real cutting horse show. We put an ad in several horse publications that announced we were looking for judges. We had real cutting-horse judges come to Long Island from Montana and Texas. Spectators came from all over the country to attend the first Christie Brinkley Cutting Horse Show, and we got both local and national press coverage. One of the attendees from Texas was an organizer of the National Cutting Horse Association Championships, which take place annually in Fort Worth. He told us it's one of the biggest and most exciting cutting horse events and it draws the greatest horses and riders. I told him that I would love to see it, and he said, "Not see it, I want you to compete in it?"

Well, the celebrity cutting championships were in two months, but he told me he would hook me up with the greatest trainer in Texas. That's how I met Punk Carter. I went down to Punk's ranch and he put me on this horse that turned so fast I felt like the cartoon character that runs off the cliff and continues to run before he falls. That horse shot out from underneath me, and I looked down and their was no animal beneath me, but then he shot back and I was on top of him again before I could hit the ground—that's how fast that horse was!

Punk is amazing. He does this stunt where he can ride a horse and read a newspaper while his horse's belly is moving so low and fast it is actually scraping the ground. Punk had me going to all kind of local competitions at night, competing with real, live, honest-to-goodness cowboys and cowgirls, and by day I was rounding up Red Brangus cattle in the middle of nowhere. The cutting horse originated out on the range, working with cattle, so Punk taught me how to separate

rate the bulls from the herd. It was incredible—we galloped over the range, jumping over ravines and bushes!

I rode one of Punk's champion horses when I competed in the celebrity division of the 1991 NCHA Championships, riding against the likes of Tanya Tucker, who learned to ride before she could stand, and Michael Keaton, who has his own cutting horse ranch. I came in fourth place that year, and the next year I *won* the event. The prizes included a trip to Hawaii and a hand-tooled saddle that says NATIONAL CUTTING HORSE CHAMPION. But perhaps my favorite trophy is the belt buckle. It says, *NCHA 1991 FUTURITY CELEBRITY CUTTING HORSE CHAMPION.* I wear that buckle with pride and it's amazing how that belt buckle just goes with everything, including evening gowns!

So you can see that I am totally hooked on riding cutting horses, and the only thing that has kept me temporarily out

West. We literally rode in the ruts of the wagons that carried the settlers across this vast land. We rode through a section of Wyoming and would go along these magnificent ridges tucked into canyons and across great flat lands and then suddenly duck down into another canyon and come up to a steep and shaly switchback. At night we would string our horses up at little motels along the way or even camp out under the stars, and then continue on the next day. I was riding my cutting horse Goodbar Miss, and one afternoon we had to outrun a giant thunderstorm. It was incredible.

"I LOVE NATURE AND THINK THAT THERE IS NO BETTER WAY TO SEE THE WORLD THAN FROM A HORSE'S BACK."

of the saddle is raising my two youngest children. But they have just been granted their wish of taking riding lessons. My husband, Peter, has always loved horses, and in fact he even won a Hampton Grand Prix Classic in Jumping. Although my oldest, Alexa, who has won several blue ribbons of her own, now prefers to sit at a piano bench, the rest of us are back in the saddle again.

I love nature and think that there is no better way to see the world than from a horse's back. It was truly a dream come true for me to ride part of the Oregon Trail across the Wild

I can even get a Big Sky experience right out in the Hamptons. A favorite day was when my friends and I rode out to a remote beach in Montauk for a big beach barbeque. I loaded up my red pickup with all kinds of food and sent it out to a remote beach. We would gallop our horses over the hills and across the wooded trails to meet up at our favorite beach and then light an early-evening bonfire, tell stories, and dine with our friends. With bellies full, our horses would then lead us home down the moonlit path, past the shooting stars. Summer nights just don't come any better than that.

WILLIAM DEVANE

Horses First. People Second.

WILLIAM DEVANE HAS SPENT NEARLY FORTY YEARS PORTRAYING GRIPPING CHARACTERS ON BOTH THE BIG AND SMALL SCREENS. HE STARRED AS PRESIDENT JOHN F. KENNEDY IN *The Missiles of October;* WITH DUSTIN HOFFMAN AND SIR LAURENCE OLIVIER IN *Marathon Man;* AND AS GREGORY SUMNER ON THE HIT TELEVISION SERIES *Knot's Landing.*

BUT PERHAPS DEVANE'S FAVORITE AND MOST ENDURING ROLE IS THAT OF HORSE OWNER. AT HIS HUNDRED-PLUS ACRE RANCH DEVELOPMENT IN THERMAL, CALIFORNIA, RANCHETTE OWNERS AS DIVERSE AS A BRAIN SURGEON, A ROCKET SCIENTIST, AND A PROFESSIONAL POLO PLAYER KEEP, TRAIN, AND RIDE THEIR HORSES. THE PROPERTY BOASTS MULTIPLE BARNS, ARENAS, AND PASTURES, A TRAINING TRACK, AND A SMALL LAKE. A HORSE LOVER FOR MORE THAN FIFTY YEARS, IT WAS NOT UNTIL HIS COSTARRING ROLE IN THE 2003 TNT MOVIE *Monte Walsh* THAT DEVANE FINALLY GOT TO PLAY A COWBOY.

As an actor I am always trying to invent

a back story that allows the character to do what he does on the screen, and, when I can, I try to include horses in all these back stories. My character Gregory Sumner on the series *Knot's Landing* rode because he had problems with human relationships and he related more to animals. My own relationship with horses allowed me to show a side of Sumner's character that was not immediately evident. The great acting teacher Stanislavsky called it the star pause, when the actor is on stage by himself and the audience is privy to something that the other characters don't see. My goal was to create a more likeable and human world for Sumner to live in, and one that the television audience was invited into.

For me, that came rather naturally. My mother grew up on a farm, and her brother ran a farm for a wealthy glove manufacturer in upstate New York. I would spend my summer there and trailer the horses in for the hunt. It got pretty brutal when we would go out in the Jeep, drag a dead fox behind us so that the dogs would pick up the scent, and then let the live fox out of the cage. Once I moved to California and started working consistently, I partnered with another guy, and we shared and boarded a horse at the Equestrian Center in Burbank. As my fortunes increased, so did my stable of horses, and I bought a small ranch in Sundance, Utah, and started keeping my horses there. Eventually, I found my place in Thermal.

With horse people, your house isn't what's important. What are important are your barn and other facilities as well as your horse trailer and the truck that pulls it. The sign to the entrance of my farm says WELCOME TO DEER CREEK. HORSES FIRST. PEOPLE SECOND. I live in a kind of collective, where horse

owners have purchased a ten-acre parcel of land from me and we all have access to the barns, hot walkers, round pens, and riding and polo arenas. These people don't know Gregory Sumner from Gregory Peck or Gunga Din. Their main concern is that we care for and pay attention to their horses. Horses really do come first at Deer Creek.

Horses have helped to keep me sane when I am not working, too. I'm the kind of guy who can really dwell on things, and at Deer Creek there is always something to do, always something to keep me occupied. This year I have been dividing the remaining three parcels of land into small five-acre ranches for sale, and working with all the new foals that have been born on the property. I need to keep my mind occupied, and the farm and horses help me do it.

I am also kind of an aggressive guy, and horses serve as a barometer for me—they both address that kind of behavior and help me to overcome it. There is a reason that at the turn of the twentieth century, playing polo became a test as to whether an Army officer was capable of grace under fire and therefore fit to be promoted from captain to colonel: It is very easy to lose your temper playing the game.

In fact, polo was an important part of my life until a broken shoulder, five broken ribs, and a broken wrist slowed me down. It all started during the *Knot's Landing* days when I boarded several horses at the Equestrian Center and met

in Palm Springs. Tommy Lee Jones joined us as well for one match, and we were able to raise more than $30,000 for the Bob Hope Cultural Center.

I never get tired of saddling up in the early morning and riding into the mountains near Thermal where I have my farm. My favorite horse is Louie, a great-looking bay Thoroughbred gelding. I ride him every day that I am not traveling or working. Sometimes the ride lasts for five minutes and other times for several hours, but Louie never fails to teach me a lesson about horsemanship and myself. I've always tried to live by the Will Rogers adage that has frequently been abbreviated, to the detriment of the horse. The exact words are: "I never met a man I didn't like who liked horses."

In show business, most of your life revolves around pretending. Acting is about creating something that isn't real and

"WITH HORSE PEOPLE, YOUR HOUSE ISN'T WHAT'S IMPORTANT. WHAT ARE IMPORTANT ARE YOUR BARN AND OTHER FACILITIES AS WELL AS YOUR HORSE TRAILER AND THE TRUCK THAT PULLS IT."

Stephanie Powers, who asked me to play in a celebrity polo fundraiser, Chuckers for Charity, to benefit the William Holden Wildlife Organization. I loved Three Day Eventing but had never played polo, so Stephanie gave a bunch of us a crash course in rudimentary polo skills.

For the next ten years we played together at charity events around the country under the banner Chuckers for Charity. Piaget became the sponsor, and we even played with Prince Charles in the Piaget Uplifters Cup at the Eldorado Polo Club

trying to make it believable. But with horses, there is a certain immediate level of reality; you can never lie to a horse because he won't want to be with you. It's amazing to me that I have been so deeply and passionately involved with horses for most of my life but was never cast in the movies or a television series as a cowboy until *Monte Walsh*. After twenty-five years of playing urban characters, I finally got to act with the likes of such Western greats as Tom Selleck and Barry Corbin. The line between fantasy and reality can be very fine indeed.

MORGAN FREEMAN

Love at First Ride

THREE-TIME OSCAR NOMINEE MORGAN FREEMAN PROJECTS AN AURA OF QUIET STRENGTH AND GREAT DIGNITY, MAKING HIM ONE OF HOLLYWOOD'S MOST SOUGHT-AFTER ACTORS. AS MUCH IN DE-MAND AS FREEMAN IS TODAY, HE DID NOT START RIDING HIGH UNTIL MORE THAN TWO DECADES AFTER STARTING DRAMA CLASSES AT LOS ANGELES CITY COLLEGE AND MAKING A MARK IN THE THE-ATER WORLD. RECEIVING CRITICAL ACCLAIM AND HIS FIRST ACADEMY AWARD NOMINATION FOR *Street Smart*, HIS CAREER DIDN'T REALLY TAKE OFF UNTIL 1989 WHEN HE WON THE GOLDEN GLOBE AWARD FOR BEST ACTOR IN A DRAMA AND RECEIVED HIS SECOND ACADEMY AWARD NOMINATION FOR HIS PIVOTAL ROLE IN *Driving Miss Daisy*. THEN THE TOP-QUALITY HITS JUST KEPT ON COMING: *Glory*, *The Shawshank Redemption*, *Se7en*, *Amistad*. OVER THE LAST FIVE YEARS, HE DEFINED THE ROLE OF ALEX CROSS IN *Kiss the Girls* AND *Along Came a Spider*, AS WELL AS STARRED IN *The Sum of All Fears* AND, OPPOSITE JIM CARREY, IN THE SMASH 2003 HIT *Bruce Almighty* PLAYING WHO ELSE BUT GOD. MOST RECENTLY, FREEMAN STARRED WITH ROBERT REDFORD AND JENNIFER LOPEZ IN *An Unfinished Life*.

FREEMAN'S DECISION TO GO BACK TO HIS MISSISSIPPI ROOTS CAME LATE IN LIFE AS WELL. RETURNING HOME IN THE LATE 1970S TO CARE FOR HIS AGING PARENTS, SEEING THAT BEAUTIFUL COUNTRY THROUGH GROWN-UP EYES CONVINCED HIM THAT THIS WAS THE PLACE FOR HIS REFUGE. WHEN TIME PERMITS, HE ESCAPES TO HIS 124-ACRE RANCH ON THE MISSISSIPPI DELTA, SOMETIMES FOR SEVERAL MONTHS AT A TIME. HE WILL RIDE EVERY MORNING, STARTING OFF SLOW AND WORKING HIMSELF UP TO THREE-HOUR ADRENALIN RUSH RIDES ON HIS HORSES BOSS BEHIND BARS, MISS T, GYPSY, AND SABLE. THE PEACE AND COMPLETE "ALIVENESS" THAT HORSES GIVE FREEMAN MAKES HIM FEEL, "TOTALLY LIBER-ATED AND TOTALLY ALIVE."

denly we came to a lower gate that Sable was able to jump over, but it had a tree stump in front of it so he started to slow down. After his first breaking move I thought, "Okay, he's going to jump," so I set myself in the saddle for the jump. But he didn't do what I expected.

I went over his head, and it wasn't more than three weeks after Christopher Reeve's accident. So I see myself flying in slow motion. Then, just as I am getting up, Sable jumped and gave me a little kick in the head. When I finally got standing, he was only ten feet away from me, as if to say, "We cool!" My neighbor saw the whole thing and she came running out. I had this big bruise on my chest that looked really nasty. Of course, after I realized I hadn't been crushed, my concern turned to Sable. I worried that he had landed on one foreleg and might be lame. But fortunately we were both okay, and walking home he followed me like a dog. Come to think of it, I guess he did win that day.

One of the reasons that my horses have so much spirit is that no one rides them but me. I have a staff that takes care of and grooms them, but I am the only person who gets on their backs. Sometimes it is several months before I can get back here, and horses are like athletes—if they don't train, which is essentially what happens when you ride them, they get out of shape. Once we get into a training session, I usually ride on a loose rein so if Sable wants to canter or gallop, he can. We ride for maybe a half an hour for several days in a row and then increase the pace until we both have three hours of ac-

tual hard riding. These sessions get us both back into shape, as well as back into harmony.

My desire to own a farm and horses back in Mississippi was late blooming. I left home when I was just eighteen years old and thought that it was good-bye forever. But as work got more and more demanding, Mississippi started looking better and better. In the late 1970s, I started going back home more often, as my parents were aging, and seeing the countryside through grown-up eyes I realized how beautiful it was. The prettiest time of the year is in the spring, but I frequently miss it due to my work schedule. But when there, I try to ride every day and sometimes even twice daily, even though my airplane is now a rival for my affection.

Unfortunately, I haven't ridden in a movie since *Unforgiven* in 1992, but I would really love to do another Western. The problem is that if one does come up again, I would want to ride Sable, and

"SOME MORNINGS I GET UP, SADDLE UP, AND JUST RIDE."

the production company won't let you use your own horse because of the liability. It would cost more to insure a private horse than those belonging to the movie wranglers. But my acting career is my acting career, and I don't really need to make a connection between the two.

Some mornings I get up, saddle up, and just ride. A lot of times Sable, or even one of my other horses, and I will be out there and there may be several hills, so I will walk him down and he follows me. To me this is so comforting and reassuring. This is the time that I feel totally complete, totally liberated, and totally alive. When I'm riding alone through the woods on a beautiful day, I look up at the sky and say, "God, it's a good day to die."

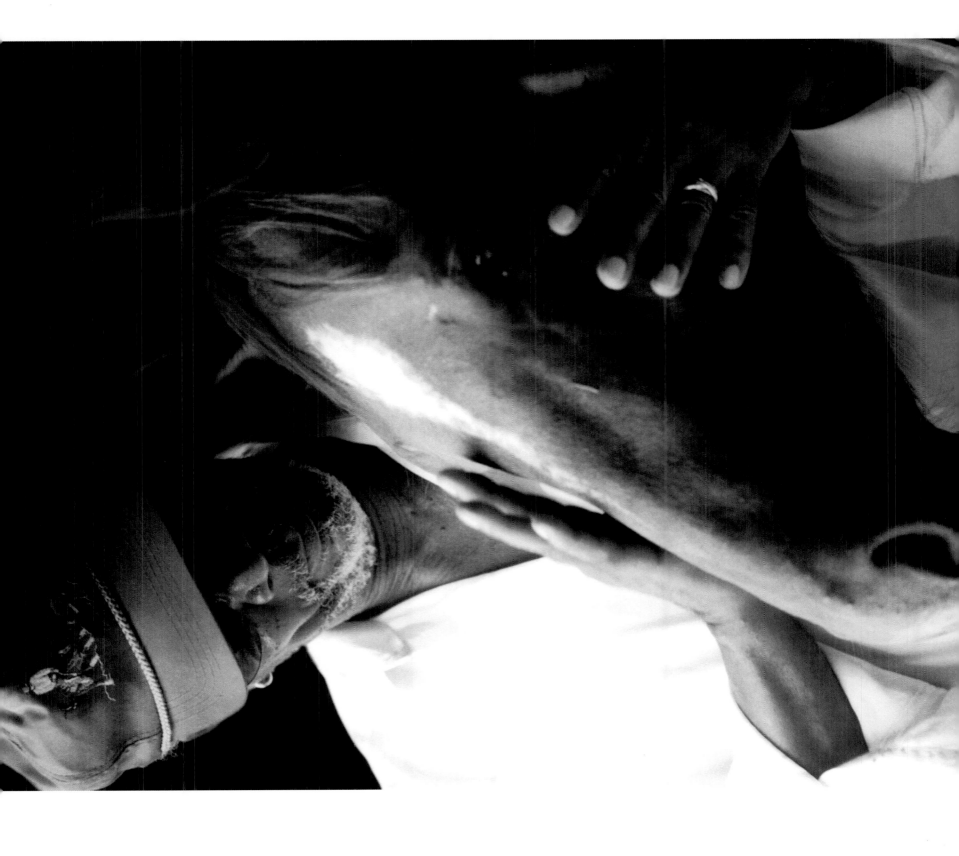

KIM NOVAK

To Have a Horse All My Own

KIM NOVAK IS TRULY A LEGEND. OVER THE COURSE OF HER CAREER, THE BLONDE BEAUTY AND TALENTED ACTRESS HAS APPEARED IN SOME OF THE MOST MEMORABLE HOLLYWOOD FILMS AND HELD THE TITLE OF THE NUMBER ONE BOX OFFICE STAR IN THE WORLD. EFFORTLESSLY MOVING FROM COMEDY TO DRAMA, NOVAK SPENT A REMARKABLE FIVE-YEAR RUN STARRING IN SUCH CLASSIC FILMS AS *The Man with the Golden Arm, Picnic, Bell, Book and Candle, The Eddy Duchin Story,* AND ALFRED HITCHCOCK'S *Vertigo.* HER BODY OF WORK IS FREQUENTLY SPOTLIGHTED IN RETROSPECTIVES AROUND THE WORLD, AND IN 2003 SHE WAS HONORED WITH THE EASTMAN (KODAK) LIFE-TIME ACHIEVEMENT AWARD FOR HER CONTRIBUTION TO FILM.

AT THE HEIGHT OF HER CAREER, NOVAK DID THE UNTHINK-ABLE—SHE MOVED OUT OF HOLLYWOOD TO BIG SUR, CALIFORNIA, WHERE SHE PURSUED HER LIFE'S GOAL OF CONNECTING WITH NA-TURE AND ANIMALS.

AFTER SEARCHING THE COUNTRY FOR "THE PERFECT HORSE," SHE FOUND HER BELOVED ARABIAN STALLION NUR JAHAN. SHE ALSO MET HER HUSBAND, EQUINE VETERINARIAN ROBERT MALLOY, ON A MIDNIGHT HOUSE CALL FOR ONE OF HER HORSES. THEY FELL IN LOVE, AND THE FOLLOWING YEAR GOT MARRIED AND SPENT THEIR HONEYMOON IN A LITTLE RED TENT UNDER THE STARS ALONG WITH THEIR TWO ARABIAN HORSES, NUR JAHAN AND TADD. AFTER YEARS OF LIVING IN CALIFORNIA, THE COUPLE MOVED TO OREGON WHERE THEY LOST BOTH HORSES TO SILICOSIS AND THEIR RIVERSIDE HOME TO FIRE; BUT THEY NEVER GAVE UP ON MAKING THEIR DREAMS COME TRUE. THEY REBUILT THEIR HOME, WITH KIM DESIGNING THE HOUSE AND APPLYING HER ARTWORK TO THE INSIDE AND OUTSIDE, WHILE BOB BUILT BRIDGES AND MILES OF TRAILS ON THEIR TWO PRIVATE ISLANDS. IT IS HERE THAT THEY RIDE THEIR TWO MORGAN HORSES, CHARLIE HORSE AND PECOS, AND DRIVE THEIR HAFLINGER HORSE HUNKA HUNKA—OR JUST LET HIM FOLLOW ALONG IN SEARCH OF NEW ADVENTURE. "HE IS ALWAYS WANTING TO BE RIGHT IN THE MIDDLE OF EVERYTHING," NOVAK SAYS OF HUNKA HUNKA. "HIS WHIMSICAL SENSE OF HUMOR NEVER FAILS TO WARM MY HEART AND MAKE ME SMILE."

My one desire while growing up

in Chicago was to have a horse and lots of wide-open spaces to ride and explore. But because of my family's financial situation, that dream was out of reach. I had my first screen test for Columbia Pictures at the age of eighteen and started working the next year, and within months I was shooting film after film, night after night, for more than a decade. I starred in more than forty films in less than twenty years. So even though I could afford a horse of my own, my schedule would not allow it; there was no time to make this kind of emotional investment. It wasn't until I decided to leave Hollywood to follow the deep need and desire to really find out who I was that horses finally came into my life.

I then took the time to find that special friend to spend my life with. I fell in love at first sight with a yearling Arabian colt in Colorado, brought him home, and named him Nur Jahan, which means Light of the Universe. I already had a dog and a cat, and I had also acquired a spunky pigmy goat, Creature, and adopted a baby raccoon, Ume, and a llama named Uno. We would have to wait two years before Nur Jahan was old enough to ride, and believe it or not, my raccoon Ume was the first to ride Nur Jahan, who never even bucked. Nur Jahan and I spent almost every day and many nights together getting to know each other and our individual boundaries, communicating in a language that we made up as we went along.

During that time I read everything I could about the preparation of horse and rider. We tested different methods,

often disagreeing with the books. Most of what I learned, Nur Jahan taught me based on trust, love, and respect. I was the only one to ever ride him without needing a bridle or saddle, even when riding among mares. I was Nur Jahan's whole life, and he was my whole life, and I often would trailer him across the country for adventures. For his fourth birthday present, my Arabian stallion got to explore the desert with a special custom-fit saddle that was made for him in New Mexico. While there, we found a small snake with a dislocated jaw and, after taking it to the zoo's veterinarian for treatment, we decided to keep him with us for the next week before heading home. When we took the snake back to the desert and re-

THE REAR EXTERIOR
OF KIM'S HOME,
SEEN FROM ACROSS
THE RIVER

leased him, at first he slid under the bushes, but while I was waiting for him to slither away, he came back to us and went up Nur Jahan's leg and wrapped himself up in my hair. Needless to say, Sincerely came home with us, where I had built a sort of indoor-outdoor house where all my animal friends could spend their quiet time in peace and harmony.

I have tried to apply the things that Nur Jahan taught me to all animals, and my life has become so very rich from all that sharing and having to look at life from my critters' different points of view. As a result, we have all gained a degree of tolerance, understanding, and appreciation for one another. I have come to believe that all things are interconnected, and I try to reflect this in my art and poetry. I am always searching to refine a language that can be understood and accepted by all, recognizing the value and values of

others, listening, and observing. I have been living these values since leaving Hollywood.

The other big love of my life is my husband, Bob. He cares for the animals as much as I do. When Bob and I moved to Oregon we bought two Morgan horses, Charlie Horse and Pecos, along with the Haflinger Hunka Hunka. He is truly a hunk, and as full of mischief as a teenaged boy, with a real lust for life.

Bob and I always had the goal of riding our horses on the Pacific Crest Trail from Mexico to Canada, but time has a way of changing goals. We now are both content to think of our barn as in Mexico as we ride our horses over Bob's bridge and through the river to our big island, which we renamed "Canada." And the best part is we can do it every week. Ah, it is a good life!

JACK PALANCE

I Will Always Be a Cowboy

THE FACE OF JACK PALANCE BECAME INDELIBLY ETCHED IN THE MINDS OF MOVIEGOERS AROUND THE WORLD WHEN HE COSTARRED AS JACK WILSON, THE BLACKER-THAN-BLACK BAD GUY IN THE CLASSIC 1953 WESTERN FILM *Shane*, FOR WHICH HE RECEIVED A BEST SUPPORTING ACTOR ACADEMY AWARD NOMINATION. AL- MOST FORTY YEARS LATER, PALANCE WAS BACK IN THE SADDLE— AND WON THE BEST SUPPORTING ACTOR OSCAR—PLAYING THE EQUALLY MEMORABLE ROLE OF CURLY IN *City Slickers*. IN BETWEEN THESE TWO GREAT ROLES CAME MORE THAN TWO HUNDRED OTHER MOVIES, IN- CLUDING *Arrowhead, Requiem for a Heavyweight, Monte Walsh,* AND *The Professionals*. AND OF COURSE

THERE WAS PALANCE'S REPRISE ROLE IN *City Slickers II: The Legend of Curly's Gold*.

NOW IN HIS EIGHTIES, PALANCE SPENDS MOST OF HIS TIME WITH HIS WIFE, ELAINE, ON THEIR TWELVE-HUNDRED-ACRE RANCH IN TEHACHAPI, CALIFORNIA. AFTER MORE THAN FOUR DECADES OF WORKING WITH HORSES FOR BOTH BUSINESS AND PLEASURE, PALANCE'S APPRECIATION FOR THEIR BEAUTY IS REFLECTED IN RARE HORSE BRONZES, EQUINE PAINTINGS, AND THE TWENTY-FOOT PEGASUS SCULPTURE THAT GRACE THE INSIDE OF THEIR RANCH HOUSE. OUTSIDE, THEIR FOUR HORSES ARE STILL RIDDEN BY ELAINE AND THE GRANDCHILDREN AND ENJOYED EVERY DAY BY PALANCE.

It's been more than seven years

since I really saddled up, but I love horses just the same. We still have four or on our property, including the Palomino that we bought from Jack Lilly, who was the head wrangler on both *City Slickers* movies. I bought that horse after we finished filming *City Slickers II: The Search for Curly's Gold*. He is probably twenty-two years old now, and we call him BJ, as his full name is Bon Jovi. BJ is the greatest horse in the world. You can put your grandmother and grandkids on top of him—a calm, good-natured, and good-working horse that could still be used on the ranch today.

I grew up in eastern Pennsylvania and didn't ride in high school or even in college. My love of horses actually coincided with my acting career. Director George Stevens called me in Florida, where I was doing a little theater, and he asked me if I rode. This was for a part in the movie *Shane*. Well, I lied and said, "Oh, yes, I do ride," never having been on a horse before. So I went to Hollywood and finally got on a horse I didn't know how in the hell to get it started! George came over to me and said, "Hey, you're the guy who says he knows how to ride and has been doing it a long time, huh?"

So I told George that at least from then on I was going to be riding for a long time. It was an absolutely delightful experience working with him and Alan Ladd. I played Jack Wilson in the movie and picked up riding pretty fast. This was the time that I really fell in love with horses.

Early in my career I never went looking for horses to own or ride, but rather roles in which I would ride horses. Of course, there is only so much acting that a cowboy can do. Even now I watch John Wayne on television and think, "My God, he won the Academy Award for a Western." But I did truly have some wonderful parts over the years where I got to ride a horse. When I did a film called *The Horsemen* with Omar Sharif, I was given an absolutely majestic black horse and rode him like the devil in the desert. By the time the filming had ended, I was one with that horse. In *City Slickers* I rode a big, red, cantankerous horse, but I tried hard not to let him get the better of me. A great moment in that movie was Billy Crystal and me sitting around the campfire singing "Tumbling Tumble Weed." I was so pleased to be cast in both the *City Slickers* movies, and I enjoyed working with Billy so much, that winning the Academy Award was just a plus. There was also a film that I did called *Arrowhead* with Charlton Heston where I played an Indian. I did a lot of bareback riding in that one, and riding bareback creates a total connection with a horse.

It has been wonderful to be able to live the cowboy lifestyle. In 1964, when I brought my big ranch in Tehachapi, as many as sixteen horses were running in the pasture. The whole ambience was of a working ranch. Elaine and I wanted a place where we could have horses and cattle, and so we purchased twelve hundred acres that included the a

"SOME OF THE WORLD'S MOST BEAUTIFUL STATUES, SCULPTURES, AND HISTORICAL BUILDINGS HAVE INCORPORATED OR FEATURED HORSES."

"I AM STILL A COWBOY IN MY HEART AND MIND."

"ELAINE AND I WANTED A PLACE WHERE WE COULD HAVE HORSES AND CATTLE, SO WE PURCHASED TWELVE HUNDRED ACRES."

main ranch house, a small historic adobe house, several outbuildings, a mobile home for the wranglers, a barn, and fencing. From 1978 to 1994, Elaine and I would frequently saddle up when I wasn't working and ride across our land. When we got back she would say, "This was so fabulous, we should do this every day."

Though I don't ride much anymore, I can still appreciate the role that horses have played in both art and architecture. Some of the world's most beautiful statues, sculptures, and historical buildings have incorporated or featured horses.

And from a plain enjoyment standpoint, Elaine and I really appreciated the recent animated movie *Spirit: Stallion of the Cimarron*, with all those beautiful horses roaming free and galloping across the plains.

We now have four older horses, and we plan to keep them here until the ends of their lives. Bon Jovi has been here almost ten years. Fiesta is a registered Pinto that we bought when she was two and a half from a man who rode in parades; her breeding is Morgan, Arab, and even a little Fox Trotter, so she has a very good gait. The other three are geldings. Wilding is a horse that we bred ourselves with one of our favorite mares, Vangie; our daughter Brooke is married to Michael Wilding Jr., Elizabeth Taylor's son, and we named him Wilding to have part of them near us. He is seventeen years old and came from Smooth Jet, a very famous Paint stal-

lion. The breeder guaranteed a live foal and color, but we call Wilding "the Paint who ain't" because he doesn't have any color at all, but he is a fabulous horse. When he was born, Elaine asked if the color would come later, but Smooth Jet's breeder said that he didn't think so.

Bronco Billy is a very strange name for an Arab. He belonged to Jack Consel, who rode him every New Year's Day in the Rose Parade for many years. As Jack started to get elderly and couldn't really ride any more, Elaine and I offered to bring Billy to what we called Palance Camp. We brought

him out here four years ago and he was the first Arab on the ranch. He has worked out just great with the other horses and is very exciting to ride. So you see that the horses that come here, come here to stay.

Having this ranch and horses always available has been a very good thing for our family. Our granddaughter Lily has been on a horse since she was less than a year old, and when we bought Bon Jovi, she was seven or eight years old. He became her horse, and Lily learned to jump really well and entered and won several competitions in some dressage events on the novice level. Of course, Bon Jovi is too quiet for her now, but Lily has turned into a great little rider, and she and Elaine ride together almost every time she comes to the ranch. As for me, I will probably never star in another Western, but I am still a cowboy in my heart and mind.

DENNIS QUAID

Loving the Way the World Looks on Horseback

AFTER STARRING IN THE DISNEY FAMILY HIT *The Parent Trap* IN 1998, CHARISMATIC LEADING MAN DENNIS QUAID CHANGED CHARACTER COMPLETELY TO TAKE ON DECIDEDLY ADULT ROLES IN SUCH CRITICALLY ACCLAIMED FILMS AS *Traffic* AND *Far from Heaven*, FOR WHICH HE RECEIVED A GOLDEN GLOBE AWARD NOMINATION FOR BEST SUPPORTING ACTOR. THIS KIND OF VERSATILITY HAS DEFINED QUAID'S LONG CAREER. WITH MORE THAN FIFTY MOVIES TO HIS CREDIT, HE HAS NEVER BEEN ONE TO BE TYPECAST.

QUAID'S CAREER TOOK OFF WITH THE CLASSIC *Breaking Away* AND HAS CONTINUED FOR MORE THAN TWENTY-FIVE YEARS

WITH SUCH POPULAR FAVORITES AS *The Big Easy, Flesh and Bone, Great Balls of Fire!, Innerspace, Frequency,* AND THE SURPRISE SLEEPER HIT OF 2002, *The Rookie.* BORN IN HOUSTON, TEXAS, PERHAPS IT'S NATURAL THAT QUAID WOULD EVENTUALLY APPEAR IN A NUMBER OF WESTERNS. IN 1980 HE AND HIS BROTHER RANDY STARRED ALONGSIDE SEVERAL OTHER "COWBOY" BROTHERS, INCLUDING STACY AND JAMES KEACH, DAVID, KEITH, AND ROBERT CARRADINE, AND NICHOLAS AND CHRISTOPHER GUEST IN THE DARK AND UNCONVENTIONAL *The Long Riders.* FOURTEEN YEARS LATER HE DELIVERED A REMARKABLE PERFORMANCE AS THE CONSUMPTIVE DOC HOLLIDAY IN THE KEVIN COSTNER–DIRECTED *Wyatt Earp.* HITTING THE TRAIL AGAIN IN 2003, QUAID DID SOME SERIOUS RIDING AS SAM HOUSTON IN *The Alamo,* DIRECTED BY JOHN LEE HANCOCK.

WHILE STILL VERY MUCH A PART OF HOLLYWOOD, QUAID IS PERHAPS MOST AT HOME RIDING ACROSS HIS SPECTACULAR AND REMOTE SIX-HUNDRED-ACRE RANCH OUTSIDE OF LIVINGSTON, MONTANA.

Even though I always liked horses,

my early riding experiences were limited to summer camp and dude ranches that my family would visit. It wasn't until I grew up and started to ride in some of my movie roles that I really began to learn about and appreciate these fabulous animals. Over the course of several months of filming, I could have a relationship with one horse and learn how to communicate with him on a daily basis.

The Long Riders was a very physical period Western where I and seven other actors, including my brother Randy, spent a lot of time on horseback. Fifteen years later, I did *Dragonheart*, and the experience was a true education for me with horses. I rode this hot Croatian horse that had never been in a movie before, and he was just fine until the crew yelled, "Rolling!" I'm not sure if it was the sound or the frequency of the camera, but he would freak out every time he heard the word "Rolling!" And I had to gallop across wheat fields with the reins in my mouth, shooting a bow and arrow.

In *The Alamo* I rode an amazing horse as well. He was not your typical trail pony but actually a trick pony that had competed in lots of rodeos and horse shows. His name was Paris and he was a little bit hard to handle because he was always fidgeting. Paris was pure white and would rear way up whenever he was given the cue. That horse was hot, loved to run,

"You get to experience the sound of your own heartbeat and the sense of silence that is so important to us all."

At my place in Montana I kind of consider the horses my puppies. They are sweet kids and I love having them around for myself and anyone else who wants to ride. Friends will come out from Los Angeles or New York who have not been around or ridden before, and it is good to put them on horse that knows how to take care of them. My horses are all well-mannered and gentle guys, but I do keep my gray Quarter Horse Ghost just for me, as he is a little hotter than the rest. We also seem to have a deeper connection than I have with my other horses. I have only had Ghost for a year and a half and came to find out that he has cancer under his tail. He is doing fine right now, but eventually I'm going to have to put him out to pasture on the ranch.

My son Jack is learning how to ride on a big black gelding named Bubba. I have a neighbor who has some cattle, and sometimes we go and push them out into a field or up into another pasture. He is turning into a real little cowboy, Jack, and this has become a whole new way for me to be a kid again.

sit in the saddle than run beside me, and ride into the back part of the property. In Montana there is a shift change early in the morning—I'll be running along on my horse and I'll see a lot of nocturnal animals still awake, along with those just coming out into the early morning sun. Everything is quiet. It puts me in a meditative place where I'm just glad to be alive. I'm able to come out of my head and my little Hollywood world and expand my mind to take in the whole valley. The first day or two I'm out at the ranch I always ask myself, "What am I going to do here?" But then a couple days later I can't imagine leaving. Time seems to stand still, and when I have been up here all by myself, two weeks can go by without me even going outside the gate.

I love the way the world looks on horseback, the way it moves by. You get to know what the real important stuff is all about. It's not about what we go through every day that seems to be screeching in your ears. That disappears, and you get to experience the sound of your own heartbeat and the sense of silence that is so important to us all.

but unfortunately he didn't want to stop, and it was a little scary when I was out there in a field and the cameras were rolling. At times the sun would be going down and I had to hold Paris in place while four hundred muskets and a couple of cannons would be going off all around us. I couldn't blame him for wanting to run, but we had to stay in character, charge across the field, and get the shot.

Part of the horse experience for me is catching, grooming, and saddling them before I ride. I'm very hands-on. It's all part of the relationship that I have with my horses. As a matter of fact, one of my favorite things to do is to go outside and just hang with them and see how they interact with one another.

I like getting up in the morning, rounding up my two chocolate Labs and little dog Clyde, who would much rather

ROBERT REDFORD

Of the West

HE'S ONE OF HOLLYWOOD'S MOST ENDURING LEADING MEN. YET, WHEN YOU CONSIDER HIS MANY OTHER TALENTS—RENOWNED FILMMAKER, COMMITTED CONSERVATIONIST, PASSIONATE HORSEMAN—IT'S OBVIOUS THAT ROBERT REDFORD IS TRULY ONE OF A KIND.

AFTER A DECADE OF FILM, STAGE, AND TELEVISION EXPERIENCE, REDFORD COSTARRED WITH PAUL NEWMAN AND KATHARINE ROSS IN A BRILLIANT TURN AS THE SUNDANCE KID IN THE CLASSIC AMERICAN WESTERN *Butch Cassidy and the Sundance Kid.* BECOMING BOX-OFFICE GOLD IN THE 1970S, HE WENT ON TO STAR IN SUCH RENOWNED FILMS AS *The Candidate, The Way We Were, The Sting, Three Days of the Condor, All the President's Men,* AND *The Electric Horseman.* AS COMFORTABLE BEHIND THE CAMERA AS HE IS IN FRONT OF IT, REDFORD'S DIRECTORIAL DEBUT, *Ordinary People,* WON HIM THE ACADEMY AWARD FOR BEST DIRECTOR IN 1981. THIRTEEN YEARS LATER HE EARNED ANOTHER BEST DIRECTOR NOMINATION FOR *Quiz Show.*

CONSTANTLY SEEKING NEW CHALLENGES, REDFORD LAUNCHED THE NONPROFIT SUNDANCE INSTITUTE TO PROMOTE INDEPENDENT FILMMAKING IN THE EARLY 1970S AND, TEN YEARS LATER, THE SUNDANCE FILM FESTIVAL, WHICH HAS GROWN TO BECOME ONE OF THE MOST PRESTIGIOUS FESTIVALS IN THE WORLD.

HE HAS BEEN A CONSISTENT, EFFECTIVE, AND IMPORTANT VOICE ON ENVIRONMENTAL ISSUES FOR MORE THAN THIRTY YEARS. AND ALL THE WHILE, HE HAS CONTINUED HIS ON-SCREEN WORK IN SUCH FILMS AS *Out of Africa* AND, MORE RECENTLY, *Spy Game,* AS WELL AS ACHIEVING SUCCESS BEHIND THE CAMERA, DIRECTING SUCH FILMS AS *A River Runs Through It,* A MOVING FAMILY DRAMA SET IN THE SPECTACULAR WESTERN LANDSCAPES OF MONTANA.

IN 1998, REDFORD WAS ABLE TO COMBINE HIS PASSION FOR BOTH FILMMAKING AND HORSES WHEN HE ADAPTED NICHOLAS EVANS'S HIT NOVEL *The Horse Whisperer.* HE DIRECTED THE FILM

AND ALSO STARRED AS TOM BOOKER, A HORSE GENTLER IN MONTANA WHO HELPS BOTH PEOPLE AND HORSES HEAL. CONTINUING HIS WORK IN WIDE-OPEN SPACES, REDFORD HAS MOST RECENTLY TEAMED UP WITH JENNIFER LOPEZ IN *An Unfinished Life,* ABOUT A RANCHER WHO TAKES IN HIS URBAN DAUGHTER-IN-LAW AFTER HIS SON DIES.

ALWAYS CONTENT TO RETURN TO HIS OWN EXTRAORDINARY RANCH IN SUNDANCE, UTAH, FOR SOME QUALITY TIME WITH HIS SIX HORSES, INCLUDING A BELOVED PALOMINO MARE NAMED CHARM, ROBERT REDFORD EMBODIES THE HEART AND SOUL OF *People We Know, Horses They Love.*

There were no horses in the poor

Los Angeles neighborhood where I grew up, except on the movie screen. My first time on a real horse was when I was five or six. I admit it was just a guy dragging me around the ring at a pony ride, but it was instant love. I asked if I could take the reins, but the guy told me it was against the rules, that he had to lead me. After several times around the ring I once again asked to take the reins. He reluctantly agreed but insisted on walking with me. Several more times around and I pleaded to go around by myself. Worn down, he let me, and I walked around the ring twice. Spotting an opening and seeing freedom on the other side, the pony and I took our chance and rode out. Of course the guy freaked out and brought me back inside. I might have given him a bad day, but it was my first taste of freedom on horseback, and it stayed with me.

By the time I was twelve or thirteen years old, a bunch of guys and I would frequent Will Rogers State Park and ride. Even though we had no clue what we were doing, we would race and spin and push each other around, me with my reins dragging on the ground and holding onto the horn. Someone asked me, "What the hell are you doing with the horn?" My best trick at the time was to make the horse go wild and take tight turns at a gallop, so my phony little excuse for using the horn was that it made the horse go faster.

My next memory of horses involves a cross-country trip

with my family traveling to New England to see my grandparents when I was fifteen. We were packed in the car and I was half-crazed with boredom. On the way home we stayed in Estes Park, Colorado, at a place that had stables; my family continued back to California, but my independent streak was deeply rooted at that point, and I decided to stay. I did any odd jobs that I could find, including grooming and caring for the horses. It was a different experience than my wild riding in Will Rogers Park, since I didn't really get to ride until the end of the day when everyone else was finished. Then I would take one of the horses and go out on my own for an hour or so. This was the start of a new relationship with horses for me. I was no longer acting like a yahoo cowboy without a clue. I developed a connection with horses, an appreciation that went beyond the satisfaction of riding horseback.

Early on, my career kept me mainly in an urban environment, but I still loved to climb mountains and surf and do physical things out in nature. I was living in New York, raising a family, but I knew that I had to live at least part of my life in the West because I was of the West. So I tried to balance things by buying two acres here in Utah for just $500 and deciding to create another dimension to my life. Back in those days, Utah was off the map—there was nothing here. I built my own cabin and learned the land by riding horseback with the sheepherders. To me, sheepherders were the fathers and engineers of this country because they did their job by in-

"I DEVELOPED A CONNECTION WITH HORSES,

AN APPRECIATION THAT WENT BEYOND THE SATISFACTION OF RIDING HORSEBACK."

"I APPRECIATED THAT A HORSE IS THE BEST WAY,
OTHER THAN ON YOUR OWN TWO FEET,
TO EXPLORE YOUR ENVIRONMENT."

stinct, by experience. So I bought my first horse and rode along with them. The deeper we went into the country, the more I appreciated that a horse is the best way, other than on your own two feet, to explore your environment.

Naturally, then, I wanted to do my own riding when I landed leading roles in my first Westerns, *Tell Them Willie Boy Is Here* and *Butch Cassidy and the Sundance Kid.* I was always very critical as a kid watching movies when the actor was obviously not doing his own stunts, so it was important for me to do my own. This meant that I had to spend more and more time with horses and get really good on their backs. It's one thing to ride casually, but to do some of the stunts that are required and to come across on camera as being in control, you have to be more than comfortable in the saddle. I've been lucky in that I've worked with some wonderful animals.

For example, I did all my own riding in *The Electric Horseman,* too. In that movie there was a scene where I had to ride along a culvert that dropped off from either side, with cop cars and even a helicopter in pursuit. I was on this incredible horse called Rising Star, who was so fast and fired up. I got on him and we both hooked in. With the helicopter pulling away, I had to go so fast that my nose and the horse's nose were almost equal. Through that experience with Rising Star I learned what it feels like to push yourself to the max and to get the max out of the animal you're on. After the filming was over, I bought Rising Star and kept him for eighteen years on my property until he died. He is buried here.

Horses have taught me a kind of meditation that's possible when you're acting as one and communicating instinctively without words. It's all about mutual respect and discipline. That's what I find so special about the movie *The*

Horse Whisperer. For me it was a chance to demonstrate my own particular affinity for horses, but the film is also about a way of life out West whose disappearance is sad but inevitable. Things come and go, and one of the things becoming obsolete is the ranching industry the way it used to be, and I wanted to document that. Still, at the heart of the story is a man whose sensitivity toward a horse, Pilgrim, could not only heal him but also heal the people around him.

Each of these experiences has led me into a deeper and deeper understanding of horses, until they became an integral part of my life. I have six horses now at Sundance, and I'm partial to Palominos. If you've ever gotten to know a horse, then you know that color isn't a consideration in their temperament, and yet as a kid I used to love to watch Roy Rogers ride his Palomino, Trigger, off into the sunset. I dreamed of having a horse just like that. When I was making *Ordinary People,* we filmed a scene in Apple Valley, California, where Roy and Dale Evans retired. It was such a thrill when Roy invited me out to his amazing ranch full of artifacts of his and Dale's cowboy life.

Coming to Utah so many years ago has made me appreciate this vastness. One particularly rewarding horse-riding adventure was a month-long journey I made from Montana down to southern Utah on the old Outlaw Trail that Butch Cassidy (the Sundance Kid) and the Hole-in-the-Wall Gang rode in the late 1880s. A *National Geographic* magazine photographer accompanied us, and I documented the ride in a thirty-page cover story for the magazine, which I later extended into a book called *The Outlaw Trail.* What I learned then, and what I continue to marvel at, is how wild and free this land was and still can seem from the back of a horse.

PRO AND SHOW

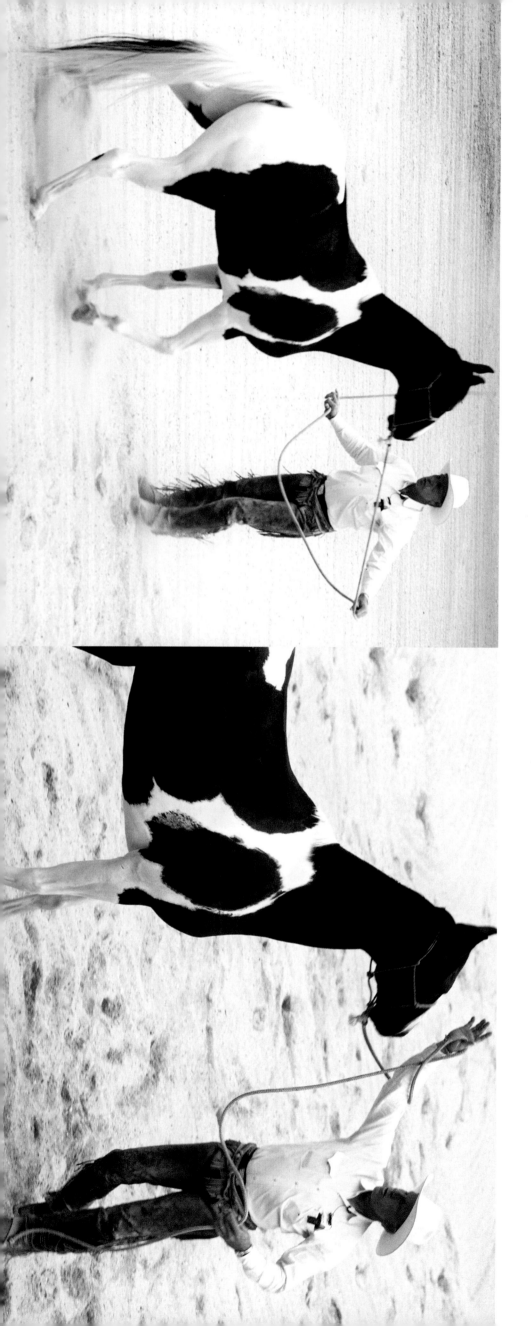

BUCK BRANNAMAN

A Better Way with Horses

"BUCK BRANNAMAN IS PART OF A LINEAGE OF SKILLED HORSEMEN,
AND FOR THE HORSES HE WORKS WITH, IT IS ABOUT TRUST
AND UNDERSTANDING, NOT SUBMISSION."
—ROBERT REDFORD

NEARLY EVERY WEEK OF THE YEAR, BUCK BRANNAMAN IS ON THE ROAD, CONDUCTING HORSEMANSHIP CLINICS IN WHICH HE TEACHES HORSE OWNERS HOW TO BETTER UNDERSTAND AND WORK WITH THEIR ANIMALS SO THEY CREATE A RELATIONSHIP BASED ON TRUST AND RESPECT RATHER THAN FORCE. BRANNAMAN'S ABILITY FOR STARTING YOUNG HORSES OFF RIGHT AND REFORMING TROUBLED HORSES HAS BECOME LEGENDARY; THE MAIN CHARACTER IN THE BEST-SELLING BOOK AND MOVIE *The Horse Whisperer* WAS BASED LARGELY ON HIM. BRANNAMAN SERVED AS AN EQUINE CONSULTANT ON THE FILM AND WORKED WITH ROBERT REDFORD ON THE MORE DIFFICULT FEATS OF HORSEMANSHIP. AND BECAUSE BRANNAMAN'S HORSE PET LOOKED VERY MUCH LIKE THE ONE DESCRIBED IN NICHOLAS EVANS'S BOOK—

BOTH WERE CHESTNUT IN COLOR, AND THE SLIGHT DIFFERENCE IN THEIR FACIAL MARKINGS WAS CAMOUFLAGED WITH HAIR AND MAKEUP—PET ALSO APPEARED IN THE FILM AS THE TROUBLED AND DAMAGED HORSE PILGRIM.

WHAT MAKES BRANNAMAN'S OWN STORY SO EXTRAORDINARY IS THE PAINFUL AND FREQUENTLY VIOLENT ROAD HE HAD TO TRAVEL BEFORE UNDERSTANDING THAT USING BODY LANGUAGE AND COMMUNICATION INSTEAD OF PHYSICAL FORCE IS THE WAY FOR HORSE AND RIDER TO ACHIEVE A TRUE UNION. GROWING UP WITH AN ABUSIVE FATHER, BRANNAMAN AND HIS BROTHER OFTEN FEARED THEY WOULDN'T LIVE THROUGH THE NIGHT. AFTER HE WAS RESCUED BY A FOSTER FAMILY, BRANNAMAN FOUND HIS CALLING—AND SALVATION—IN WORKING WITH HORSES.

There were those amazing men who could see into the creature's soul

and soothe the wounds they found there.

—THE HORSE WHISPERER

I learned from my dad that violence

was not the way to work with horses. It was one of the few things he would teach me.

My dad was like an awful lot of backyard horse owners in the 1960s who didn't know anything about horses but felt it was macho to abuse them. He must have gotten advice from some self-proclaimed horse trainer who was very strict and severe with horses. It was the same way that my dad treated us kids.

One of my most painful and vivid memories growing up was what my dad did to my brother's mare, which he wanted to train to be a roping horse. She was whinnying for another horse and kind of having a hard time because her equine buddy had just been moved off of our property. The mare was lonesome for her friend and that made my dad a little crazy; he didn't understand that she was just feeling insecure. We were working on a fence and dad got so mad that he threw a claw hammer at this mare from about fifty feet away from her. I don't know how in the hell it happened, but the head of the

hammer hit her right between the eyes and fractured her skull. The blow didn't kill her, but she always had a dent in her forehead, and every time I would pet that mare it would remind me about the kind of person my dad really was. Needless to say, she never made it into trick roping, and eventually my dad sold her.

We were living in Idaho at the time, and even at age seven or eight that one incident made a huge impression on me. I knew that this was no way to work with or treat horses, and I vowed to do it differently. It goes back to the basic instinct of nurturing; I knew in my heart that it was wrong to try and teach any living thing through that kind of violence. There wasn't much that I could do about the abuse at the time, as I was as much a captive as that horse was, but I do remember thinking that there had to be a different way to live. Fortunately, years later I was able to find out what that felt like.

I think that my father was a failed performer at heart. He really wished that he could have been the famous trick roper Monty Montana, but instead he tried to live that dream through my brother and me. We started doing rope tricks when I was three and my brother was five, and from that point on you either practiced rope tricks or you got whipped. As I was terrified of my dad, trick roping became a way of pleasing him, and even though we always fell short of his expectations, my brother and I began to enjoy the applause and attention that an audience gave us. It got into our blood. We believed that the people in the audience cared about us, and this was something that we needed desperately at the time.

As my life progressed, I ended up living with a foster family in Montana. My mom passed away when I was thir-teen and my brother and I were removed from our home by the state when dad became more and more abusive. We ended up with the Shirlee family, and Forrest, my foster dad, was everything I wished my biological dad had been. Forrest had a ranch and was the first real cowboy I had ever been around. He looked like he was right out of the movies. My foster dad was my inspiration for becoming a good horse hand and an even better cowboy.

The Shirlees didn't have much money, so my brother and I did work around the ranch to help pay for our clothes and food. One morning Forrest gave me a bit of advice that pushed me into the horse world in a very strong way. He said, "Kid, if you learn how to ride a colt and shoe a horse, you'll always get to eat." Shoeing a horse at the ranch could become a real Western event, as most of the horses were either rank or renegade, and it didn't take me too long to figure out that I wanted to be on top of the animal instead of underneath it. I started riding colts and young horses, and that too was a Western event, because my foster dad didn't know some of the new methods. But we did the best we could to get along with them, and that is where my career starting young horses began. I ended up riding colts all through high school.

Working so hard and supporting myself as a young teen actually turned out to my advantage. When I graduated from high school at barely seventeen, I had been getting paid for riding young horses and, in a sense, had my own business. By the time I was eighteen I was running a big horse operation at Three Forks Ranch at the headwaters of the Missouri River. The ranch was affiliated with renowned horse gentler Ray Hunt, and its horse program was patterned after his methods. Because of my instinctual ability with horses, the

"THERE ARE LOTS OF WAYS TO MAKE A LIVING, BUT SHARING WITH OTHERS THE HEALING THAT HAPPENED TO ME—THAT'S SOMETHING SPECIAL."

ranch sent me to Ray's clinics, and he changed my life in terms of working with horses. Ray set me up for a career that I couldn't even begin to envision then.

Basically Ray Hunt took what another extraordinary horseman, Tom Dorrance, taught him and used it to teach owners how to understand their horses. The philosophy is that to teach a horse you need to do it in such a way that the horse gets to help make up the rules. You are trying to get your idea to become the horse's idea but not force it on him—it has to be his choice. Tom believed that by making the wrong choice difficult and the right choice easy with consistent reinforcement, the horse will choose the right thing to do most all of the time. It is also important to have a feel for and love for the horse. Thank goodness we live in a time when a man can really love his horses, be friends with his horses, and not be considered a sissy.

My work with colts in Montana made me to want to help people understand their horses, but I was absolutely terrified of speaking in front of groups. My first real clinic was at an indoor arena near Four Corners, Montana. I was just twenty-two years old, and I don't know that the attendees learned a hell of a lot because I was trying to imitate Ray and should have just been myself. It really bothered me that I wasn't able to speak to those people comfortably, so I decided to keep holding clinics at my place on the weekends, to practice. Some weekends I would get twenty

people; at $10 for the afternoon, that was big, big money for me. After a year or two I was more comfortable and more effective in my teaching technique, and I started to realize that working with both horses and people might turn into something that a fellow could do to support himself. Gradually, through word of mouth, I built up a following, and twenty years later I am on the road nine to ten months a year. Never a week goes by that a least one person doesn't draw me aside after class and tell me that my clinic has profoundly changed their life.

For me, meeting Forrest and Ray brought me from absolute despair to prosperity, not in the financial but in the emotional sense. There are lots of ways to make a living, but sharing with others the healing that happened to me—that's something special.

I've been a horseman for most of my life now, yet that magic moment still happens every time I get on a horse. Tomorrow morning I am going to ride out on the ranch and gather about two hundred head of steers and sort them out for an upcoming clinic. The hills are green, the sun will be shining brightly, and I am going to have another wonderful day on one of my horses. If tomorrow is not another great horse experience, it's my own damn fault. It is sort of like being responsible for enjoying your own life. I don't put that responsibility on anybody else. I take it on myself to make every day just something that I really enjoy!

TAMI HOAG

The Joy and Challenge of Dressage

"Early in my life I came to the conclusion that my spirituality was something uniquely and privately my own, something I could find deep within a small, quiet space in the very center of my being . . . I find that place within me when I am on a horse."

—FROM *DARK HORSE* BY TAMI HOAG

TAMI HOAG HAS BEEN ENTERTAINING AND THRILLING READERS EVER SINCE THE PUBLICATION OF HER FIRST NOVEL IN 1988. HER BOOKS ARE ACTION-PACKED AND FAST-PACED, OFTEN FEATURING NO-NONSENSE HEROINES RANGING FROM COPS TO COURT RE-PORTERS. A PROLIFIC WORKAHOLIC, SHE HAS WRITTEN NEARLY A DOZEN BESTSELLERS IN THE LAST DECADE, INCLUDING *Ashes to Ashes, Dust to Dust, Dark Horse,* AND *Kill the Messenger.*

RIDING BEFORE SHE WAS WRITING, HOAG IS A GRAND PRIX DRESSAGE RIDER WITH THREE MAGNIFICENT EUROPEAN WARM-BLOOD HORSES SHE BOARDS AT A FRIEND'S RANCH IN THE MALIBU MOUNTAINS. WITH HER 2002 BESTSELLER, *Dark Horse,* HER ART AND HER REALITY CROSSED PATHS. THE STORY, SET AGAINST THE GLAMOROUS BACKDROP OF HIGH-STAKES INTERNATIONAL SHOW

JUMPING COMPETITION, CENTERS ON THE KIDNAPPING OF A YOUNG WOMAN WORKING AS A GROOM. WHILE ON THE CASE, HOAG'S HEROINE, EX-COP ELENA ESTES, EXPLORES A WORLD OF PEOPLE WHO LOVE HORSES AND THE PEOPLE WHO LOVE TO EXPLOIT THE PEOPLE WHO LOVE HORSES.

For most of my life, one solid

constant has been the comfort of being with horses. When-ever I've gone through a difficult time in my life, I could always find peace and happiness with the horses and be taken out of my self-absorption. This is particularly true riding dressage because it is such an intense sport—especially at the higher levels of competition.

The relationship between horse and rider is an intimate one. For me this is particularly so between myself and my Grand Prix horse, Feliki. The Grand Prix is the highest level of competition in dressage. At this level, horse and rider must perform the most complex and difficult movements in a specific order called a test. Within the test, every movement is judged and scored on quality and correctness. This means I have to focus on everything going on with Feliki beneath me. Do I need her to be quicker? More bend or less in this movement? More left leg? Less right rein? And she has to focus on me and respond to the slightest pressure from my leg, the subtle tensing of one finger on a rein.

Dressage at this level is physically and mentally demanding, yet the picture of horse and rider should be one of absolute harmony and ease. To achieve one perfect moment in a test can come down to something so minute as the smallest shift of my weight in the saddle for the briefest flash of time. There is no room in that time to worry about a deadline or a love affair or the meaning of life. In that moment, this is the meaning of life.

I have loved horses for as long as I can remember, but I didn't have one of my own until I was nine years old. Like most parents, mine kept hoping horse craziness was just a phase, but

no. I read about horses, drew pictures of horses, dreamed about horses. My first short story was about two children who shared a black pony—a writing assignment in the third grade.

As it turned out, my first mount was a black pony. Unfortunately for me, he was an evil creature who hurled me to the ground every chance he got. But I am nothing if not determined, and that pony was eventually traded for a better pony, and suddenly we had a barn full of ponies. My father enjoyed buying and selling and trying to find a diamond in the rough. Gradually, ponies made room for Quarter Horses, and I spent my teens and twenties showing, riding Western. Riding was always my escape. I could get on a horse and go off at a canter and let go of everything else.

It wasn't until the late 1980s that I first became interested in the art and sport of dressage. Living in rural Minnesota, opportunities to pursue this new passion were limited. But I did my detective work and found Marianne Ludwig. Marianne, a well-known figure in American dressage, was my first teacher, and she kindled in me a desire not only to ride, but to understand the how and why of every moment on the horse.

About that time, my career began to take off and took precedence over everything else in my life. The way a writer makes a name is to be prolific as well as good. This meant deadline after deadline. I lost five years of riding time, and nearly lost my mind, but after those five years I was able to afford a good horse and was entitled to get my life back. I moved to Virginia horse country and said to myself, "Okay, now I'm really going to do this. I'm forty, and I don't have time to mess around."

So began my search for the perfect horse. I tried about thirty horses before I fell in love. The horse was D'Artagnon, a beautiful bright chestnut Westphalen gelding. However, he was not by any means an easy horse to ride, and I probably had no business buying him. I'd hardly ridden in half a decade and had only a rudimentary start in dressage. But when I sat on D'Artagnon, I knew he was the horse that would make me a better rider. I bought him on Valentine's Day and promptly left on a book-signing tour to promote *A Thin Dark Line.*

When I returned, I began to train with world-class dressage rider and coach Betsy Steiner. Betsy was the perfect coach for me. While other people thought I had bitten off more than I could chew, Betsy just grinned and said, "Let's do it!"

I trained six days a week, much of that time on my own, learning to apply the things Betsy was teaching me in our catch-as-catch-can lessons. It was the hardest work I've ever done in my life—physically, mentally, emotionally. And I needed to shape up fast, because I was determined to compete in a show the beginning of June. I had ten weeks, which is the blink of an eye in the dressage world. People train for years, ride at the lower levels for years. D'Artagnon and I would make our debut at Fourth Level at one of the most prestigious shows on the East Coast.

We came home with two blue ribbons and a hunger for more. By the fall I had moved up a level, to Prix St. Georges, the first of the upper levels of dressage. By the end of our second season, D'Ar and I finished fifth in the nation among amateur riders at that level.

I purchased Feliki and my younger horse, Oliver, the fall of 2000 in Holland, and spent that winter in Florida, competing with the best horses in the country. Feliki and I quickly became great partners. In our first Grand Prix together, we placed sixth in a field of experienced amateurs and professional riders. At the end of the year, Feliki and I

"My horses provide the perfect balance in my life."

were U.S. Dressage Federation amateur champions at the Intermediare II level and reserve champions at the Grand Prix.

I live in Southern California now. Betsy, who had trained me in the Los Angeles area for years before moving to Virginia, recommended I go see Lynn Cardoso, who had a ranch in the mountains above Malibu—Iron Horse Ranch. The scenery is incredible, the ranch itself a little jewel tucked back into the hills. The barn holds just fourteen horses, all of them dressage horses owned by amateur riders. Lynn has become a great and valued friend, and everyone in the barn, from the other boarders to my trainer, Aaron Wilson, and our groom, John Black, feels like family to me. They are a warm and wonderful group of people.

My most perfect experience with her was at the 2001 Palm Beach Dressage Derby. This was only my fourth Grand Prix, but Feliki and I were in the zone. Coming down that center line, I knew we had become true partners. We won the class with the highest score of all the Grand Prix rides, amateur or professional, and on the final day we were named Grand Prix Champions. I still get goosebumps when I remember it.

Oliver is my gorgeous party boy, and like most gorgeous party boys, work is not his favorite thing. But I have a weakness for gorgeous party boys, and I have hopes of making him my upper-level horse in a few years. Arli is a tall, striking, pale gray Danish warmblood with the softest, kindest eyes. He's a sensitive soul who needs the confidence of his rider/partner to coax the best from him. Arli and I will compete at the Prix St. Georges level. The European breeds excel at dressage be-

cause of their beautiful natural gaits, their size, their spirit, and bodies just built for the sport.

Sadly, I had to retire my beloved D'Artagnon due to chronic lameness in his hind legs. It broke my heart. I still cry driving home from visiting him at the small ranch where he lives. He was my first partner, and he saw me through a very difficult time in my life. And he was such a show horse! He loved the limelight. His job now is as "Uncle D'Ar" to the foals at the ranch. He seems to like that, though I suspect not nearly as much as he loved the show ring. I miss that special partnership with him very much.

My horses provide the perfect balance in my life, as they always have. My work enables me to afford my equine friends, and those friends give my life perspective. Writing a book is a very intense experience; solitary, completely absorbing. It's easy for me to get too involved with the process, to the point that every little thing about it consumes me, worries me, makes me doubt my ability. When I get like that, I know it's time to be with the horses and clear my head. They calm me and comfort me. They are my joy, refuge, therapy, salvation, and comfort. They don't know or care about writer's block or plot twists. All they want is a carrot and to be scratched and petted. They want to spend time with me just because I'm me, and they like me. The horses are always exactly who they are. They don't lie. They have no hidden agenda. They are pure souls, and their love is unconditional . . . except for that carrot thing. I think that's a pretty small price to pay for all they do for me.

U.S. EQUESTRIAN TEAM

Grand Prix Jumping

Much More than Winning a Medal

Some of the most exciting and skillful events at the summer Olympic games are the equestrian events, which include precision dressage and the grueling and difficult Three Day Eventing. But perhaps most beautiful to watch is the Grand Prix show jumping, where horse and rider soar through the air, apparently with the greatest of ease. Margie Goldstein Engle and Norman Dello Joio have mastered this skill and have competed on a combined total of three Olympic teams, spanning more than two decades. The ties that bind these two very different athletes are not only success in the winner's circle or another team medal, but lifelong love and careers being with and riding high on these magnificent animals.

At the age of forty-five, Margie Goldstein Engle is one of the most active and successful riders on the Grand Prix circuit. In November 2003, Engle won the Budweiser/AGA (American Grand Prix Association) Show Jumping Championship. She has also won the Budweiser Grand Prix Rider of the Year Award a remarkable seven times. Riding her beloved horse Hidden Creek's Perin in the 2000 Olympic Games in Sydney, Engle placed tenth in the Individual Show Jumping competition and helped the U.S. to a sixth-place team finish. She was the highest placed U.S. rider and the highest placed woman in the individual competition.

Nicknamed "Stormin' Norman" for his aggressive riding style, Dello Joio was first named to the U.S. Olympic Team in 1980, but did not compete due to the U.S. boycott. He established an American Grand Prix Association record when he rode Johnny's Pocket to five wins in 1981. Eleven years later, Dello Joio earned the Individual Bronze Medal at the 1992 Barcelona Olympics riding the chestnut gelding, Irish. Continuing to excel for the next decade, he capped his 2000 season by winning the $100,000 President's Cup at the Washington International Horse Show in Washington, D.C. Dello Joio and his cherished horse Glasgow also won the $30,000 Adequan Fiesta Day Grand Prix at the Hampton Classic in August 2003.

Margie Goldstein Engle

I have always loved animals. My parents used to tease me at a very young age that the house would be a zoo if I had my way. We lived on a lake, and when I was six or seven I made an incubator to hatch duck eggs. All animals were important to me, including horses, and even though I didn't grow up with them, a friend of mine would take me to her barn, and that is where I fell in love with these fabulous animals. I remember coming home and begging my parents to let me take riding lessons.

At first this seemed out of reach for my family, as we were not very wealthy. I knew that riding was a luxury and that lessons were expensive. But after begging and begging my parents for months, they finally said that they could afford to pay for one lesson a week. So that is how I started riding, by taking one lesson a week at Glavens Farm in Miami.

Daydream was the first horse I owned a small part of. My father helped me put together a financial package with other family members and we were able to purchase him. He was the first good Grand Prix horse that I was able to keep, and he is now twenty-two and still with me. As my Grand Prix skills and wins increased, I started to ride Salut, a great Dutch stallion and one of the best horses I ever had. Salut knew exactly what I was thinking, and he would try to please me no matter what. He still holds the record for most Grand Prix and American Grand Prix Association wins in one year.

In 2000 I started to compete on Hidden Creek's Perin, another remarkable horse, and he won the Horse of the Year in 2001 from the American Horse Show Association. That year I also placed extremely high at the Olympic trials and was chosen to go to Sydney to compete in the 2000 Summer Games. Competing in the Olympic Games is something that I had

always dreamed about, but when I first started riding it seemed out of my grasp. It was incredible to actually be in Sydney as the best individual American and also the highest place woman to ride there. It was Perin's first year of Grand Prix show jumping and he had no business being there, but I placed tenth individually with him and sixth in the team competition. He didn't have much show experience, but performed with such raw talent and jumped the big jumps so easily.

Over time, I've learned that riding is so much more than competition. You have to build a strong relationship with the animal, have goals, and both work hard together. Horses are very giving animals, and if you work with them correctly they will give everything they have for you and then some. Perin gave 100 percent during this very stressful and competitive time and performed at an Olympic level.

Norman Dello Joio

I didn't start riding until the age of fourteen, when I got a job on Long Island as a groom. I started working at a barn in exchange for lessons. Several years later I became interested in show jumping. Growing up, most boys are interested in playing team sports such as baseball and hockey and are not that interested in horses, at least in this country, because they are competing against girls and don't want to be beaten by them. But over time, I think that competitive riding and jumping balances out at the higher levels and may even become a little more male dominated at the top of the heap. Thinking back, perhaps I got interested in horses as a teenager because of all the cute girls.

I grew up in an atypical household. My father was a composer, and even though I thought of my chosen career as a creative extension of what my father was doing, I was going in a completely different direction than anybody in my family had ever gone. My family didn't really understand my choice of an equestrian career, and I became successful pretty much on my own, without a great deal of financial support. Getting into the sport worked in my favor in many ways, though, not the least of which is that I met my future wife, Jeanie, when we were both just eighteen. She was the nanny for the children of a big horse dealer who sold me a horse. It was pretty amazing, as that horse, Allegro, ended up being on the 1980 Olympic team, and with him came my wife.

Jeanie and I started a great partnership, and she supported everything that I was trying to achieve. We couldn't afford to hire stable help, so we would get up at six in the morning and muck out the stalls and pony the horses up to the ring where I would practice and give lessons. There where nights when

Jeanie and I would sleep in the barn or tack room, as we put all the money we made back into the horses. We were living on a shoestring budget, but were able to pull it all together during the late 1970s. As our business grew, people started to seek me out to ride their horses for them.

Allegro and I made the Olympic Team, but my dream of winning a medal in 1980 was not to be realized, as the United States boycotted those Olympics. During this difficult time I found out, even if it does sound like a cliché or corny, that there is truly an Olympic spirit. Many, many

NORMAN DELLO JOIO MASTERED THE 5½-FOOT JUMP TO WIN A $30,000 PURSE AT THE 2003 HAMPTON CLASSIC.

people didn't care if we were from the U.S. or what was then called Behind the Iron Curtain. It was absolutely how you related to the sport that mattered.

Twelve years later I was able to compete in Barcelona and earned the Individual Bronze, riding a wonderful chestnut gelding named Irish. He was probably the greenest and youngest horse at the Olympics, and the extent of his Grand Prix experience was at the Trials leading up to the summer Games. Throughout each phase of the Olympics, Irish performed better and better, and we ended up with the Bronze. The Olympic experience for me was also about watching and learning about other athletes who lived in the Village and meeting people from other countries and other sports and how they operated and performed in competition.

My horse of this decade is Glasgow, and over the last three years we've had several important Grand Prix wins.

"MY FAMILY DIDN'T REALLY UNDERSTAND MY CHOICE OF AN EQUESTRIAN CAREER."

During the mid-1990s, I started to slow down a bit and concentrated on training riders and working with young horses. But when I heard about Glasgow, I went to Scotland to see him and immediately knew that he was the next horse for me. I went home with his video in my bag and convinced six other people to come up with some cash and we syndicated Glasgow. His first big win was at the Grand Prix in Culpeper (Virginia) in 1999 and he has been winning ever since.

Being chosen to compete on two Olympic Teams has been great, but that is not what motivates me nearly as much as a continuing career in the sport. I love all aspects of equine competition; for me it's my job, the way I feed my family. I know I'm lucky because not many people can make a good living doing what they are so passionate about. The last twenty-five years have been a really good time, and I am looking forward to the next twenty.

JULIE KRONE

Resurrection

JULIE KRONE IS AN AMERICAN ORIGINAL. AS A WOMAN COMPETING ON EQUAL TERMS WITH MEN IN THE ROUGH-AND-TUMBLE WORLD OF THOROUGHBRED RACING, SHE HAS SUCCEEDED BEYOND ALL REASONABLE EXPECTATIONS. IN 1993 SHE BECAME THE FIRST WOMAN TO WIN A TRIPLE CROWN EVENT, WHEN SHE WAS VICTORIOUS ABOARD COLONIAL AFFAIR IN THE BELMONT STAKES. IN 2003 SHE BECAME THE FIRST WOMAN TO WIN A MILLION-DOLLAR RACE, WHEN SHE TOOK THE PACIFIC CLASSIC WITH CANDY RIDE. LATER THAT SAME YEAR SHE BECAME THE FIRST WOMAN TO WIN A COVETED BREEDERS' CUP RACE ON THE NATIONALLY TELEVISED CHAMPIONSHIP DAY WHEN SHE RODE HALFBRIDLED IN THE MILLION-DOLLAR BREEDERS' CUP JUVENILE FILLIES. NEARING THE END OF THE 2003 SEASON, KRONE REACHED THE 3,700 MARK IN CAREER WINS, A LEVEL ACHIEVED BY NO OTHER WOMAN AND RELATIVELY FEW MEN.

KRONE WAS HONORED IN 1993 BY THE WOMEN'S SPORTS FOUNDATION AS THE INDIVIDUAL SPORTSWOMAN OF THE YEAR. IN 1999 SHE WAS SELECTED FOR MEMBERSHIP IN THE NATIONAL COWGIRL HALL OF FAME IN FORT WORTH, TEXAS. AND IN 2000, KRONE ATTAINED THE HIGHEST RECOGNITION HER SPORT CAN BESTOW WHEN SHE BECAME THE FIRST WOMAN INDUCTED INTO THE THOROUGHBRED RACING HALL OF FAME IN SARATOGA SPRINGS, NEW YORK.

BUT HER SUCCESS HAS COME AT A COST. KRONE HAS SUSTAINED A NUMBER OF INJURIES DURING HER ILLUS-

TRIOUS CAREER, SOME OF THEM SERIOUS, AND SHE TOOK A THREE-AND-A-HALF YEAR HIATUS FROM COMPETITION BEGINNING IN THE SPRING OF 1999. AT THE AGE OF THIRTY-NINE, SHE CAME BACK WITH A VENGEANCE AS THE LEADING MONEY-WINNER OF THE PRESTIGIOUS DEL MAR (CALIFORNIA) RACING SEASON.

KRONE HAS RIDDEN LITERALLY THOUSANDS OF HORSES DURING HER CAREER. NOT ONE OF THEM, HOWEVER, HAS MEANT AS MUCH TO HER AS THE THOROUGHBRED-WARMBLOOD CROSS NAMED PETER RABBIT. A TALL, HANDSOME CHESTNUT WITH A STRIKING WHITE BLAZE AND FOUR WHITE STOCKINGS, PETER RABBIT WAS BORN IN 1982, THE YEAR AFTER KRONE BEGAN HER CAREER AS A JOCKEY. HE WAS RAISED AND TRAINED BY JUDI KRONE, JULIE'S

MOTHER, AN ACCOMPLISHED RIDER AND TRAINER. PETER RABBIT WAS BARELY TWO YEARS OLD, ALREADY A HEAD-STRONG YOUNG COLT, WHEN JUDI KRONE WAS DIAGNOSED WITH TERMINAL CANCER. JUDI PERSEVERED, FOCUSING HER SKILLS ON THE DEVELOPMENT OF PETER RABBIT EVEN AS SHE BATTLED THE RAVAGES OF HER ILLNESS. TO THIS DAY, KRONE IS CONVINCED THAT PETER RABBIT BROUGHT OUT THE FIGHT IN HER MOTHER, INSPIRING HER WITH THE WILL TO SURVIVE MUCH LONGER THAN HER DOCTORS PREDICTED SHE WOULD. WHEN JUDI KRONE DIED, JUST BEFORE CHRISTMAS OF 2000, KRONE TURNED TO HER FRIEND PETER RABBIT AS AN ANCHOR IN HER TIME OF SORROW.

It was on Easter morning of 1982

when my mom called to say, "Guess what the Easter Bunny brought?" At the time, she lived in Florida, where her stable of horses included a warmblood mare and a Thoroughbred stallion by the name of It's a Gray Issue. I had bought It's a Gray Issue at a racetrack and given him to my mom for a Valentine's Day present. He was a flashy gray with a lustrous black mane and tail and a long forelock that swept dramatically down over his face. My mom and I agreed that if his first foal was a colt, he would be mine. If it was a filly, then she would belong to my mom.

Well, I got my chestnut baby boy. Mom wanted to call him Easter Stocking, but I insisted on Peter Rabbit because I knew he was going to be a jumper, and, boy, was I right. But Peter Rabbit would not have been the great jumper he was without the training that my mom gave him.

A year and a half after Peter Rabbit was born, my mom was diagnosed with cancer. She was told she had just three months to live. The cancer had been found throughout her body: in her liver, her pancreas, her ovaries, her small intestines, even at the bottom of her heart. She began treatments, including chemotherapy, but somehow my mom still had the strength to go out to the stables. Even weak with the chemo treatments, she would put the bridle on Peter Rabbit and longe him around the ring. Sometimes she would take a nap, then train him, take another nap, then train him some more.

Mom did not die in three months. In fact, she continued to train Peter Rabbit at her Florida farm for the next five years. By the time she sent him to me, he was beautifully trained to fourth-level dressage. But he was reluctant to jump.

That's when I sent Peter Rabbit to Margie Goldstein, a member of the U.S. Olympic Equestrian Team. Margie turned Peter Rabbit into the most lovely jumper you can imagine, and I have plenty of blue ribbons to prove it.

The jockey's life requires a lot of travel, but Peter Rabbit went with me everywhere: New York, New Jersey, Louisiana, Florida, Kentucky, and finally to California. He became my dearest friend, and I couldn't stand to go anywhere without him.

Peter Rabbit has more heart and more courage than most of the racehorses I have ridden. I really believe that if Peter had thumbs, he would rule the world. He is a passionate horse who would prance and sweat whenever he performed. He is a warrior, a soldier, and he possesses the strongest character I have ever been around. When Peter Rabbit was about eleven years old, I took him to a jumping clinic where there were horses from Europe valued at hundreds of thousands of dollars. Peter didn't care. My homebred horse just attacked the hills and leaped over the ditches. He galloped through the natural obstacle course with his neck arched. And when he met a jump he could not clear, he climbed over it!

Racing horses, like riding Peter Rabbit, is an exhilarating experience. The feeling is so addicting that I have been willing to accept the danger for the thrill of winning a race. At one point, though, after two very severe injuries in a short period of time, I lost my passion for the sport. At about the same time, my mom's illness became grave. Despite all her courage, I knew she did not have long to live. So, in April of 1999, I stopped riding racehorses to spend more time with her. A fighter to the end, my mom lasted four weeks longer than her doctors predicted. My brother, Donnie, and I were by her side every day.

"I KNEW THAT THE LESSONS SHE TAUGHT PETER RABBIT MEANT HE WOULD ALWAYS CARRY PART OF MY MOM INSIDE HIM."

After our mother's death, I returned to my home in California and went straight to the stables where I kept Peter Rabbit. He had missed me, for he was looking thin and he was depressed, as if he knew what our family was going through. Being so close to him for so long, at that moment in my life I could think only about how my mom bred him, raised him, and trained him as a young horse. I thought of how my mom taught me the secrets of riding, and that she had so much more to give. I knew that the lessons she taught Peter Rabbit meant he would always carry part of my mom inside him. I remembered that Easter morning phone call—"Guess what the Easter Bunny brought?"—and suddenly I realized I hadn't really cried yet over my mom's death. That's when I broke down. I sat in that stall, with Peter Rabbit at my side, and sobbed for an hour.

In November of 2002, I returned to racing just as abruptly as I had left. I missed going to the track. I missed the morning workouts. I realized that the best thing of all is just being around the horses all the time. So I decided, "Hey, I want to do this again." Sure, I'd like to ride in another Triple Crown race; maybe even win one. But no matter what happens, I love what I do every day. And even when I would have a bad day at the track, there

were times when I would come home and go for a beautiful trail ride with Peter Rabbit. A horse always seemed to hold the answer to how I was feeling. I have a sign in my kitchen that says it all: "I've spent most of my life riding horses. The rest I've just wasted."

It is the story from *The Arabian Nights* that really puts into perspective how much horses mean to me. A king is admiring the horse of a traveler, but he does not quite understand why the traveler thinks so highly of this horse.

"I see nothing unusual," the king says. "True, the mane is a handsome one. Yes, he is twice the size of the horses we keep here in the stables. His form is handsome. His eyes are bright...."

"That is not all," interrupts the traveler. "You have only to climb on his back and wish yourself anywhere in the world—and, no matter how far the distance, in a flash of time too short to count you will find yourself there. It is this, Your Highness, that makes my horse so wonderful."

That is what makes all horses so wonderful, from my own precious Peter Rabbit to the racehorses I ride for a living. No matter the horse, I have only to climb on his back and wish myself anywhere in the world. It is my relationship with these special animals that brings so much quality to every day of my life.

ALFRE WOODARD
AND MAVIS SPENCER

A Mother and Daughter's Spiritual Bond

MULTI AWARD WINNING—ACTRESS ALFRE WOODARD BROKE INTO THE ACTING SCENE IN 1983 IN A VERY BIG WAY WHEN SHE WAS NOMINATED FOR AN OSCAR FOR HER PERFORMANCE AS GEECHEE IN *Cross Creek*. HER NEXT PROFESSIONAL MILESTONE CAME IN THE MID-1980s WHEN SHE WON TWO EMMY AWARDS FOR HER RECURRING ROLES ON *L.A. Law* AND *Hill Street Blues*. CONSTANTLY PURSUING CHALLENGING AND UNCONVENTIONAL ROLES, WOODARD RECEIVED A GOLDEN GLOBE NOMINATION FOR JOHN SAYLES' *Passion Fish* AND THE TRIPLE

CROWN OF AMERICAN TELEVISION HONORS—AN EMMY, A GOLDEN GLOBE, AND A SCREEN ACTOR'S GUILD AWARD—FOR HER PORTRAYAL OF THE TITLE ROLE IN *Miss Ever's Boys*. MOST RECENTLY, SHE STARRED WITH ED HARRIS AND CUBA GOODING JR. IN *Radio*, A POIGNANT STORY OF SEVERE CHALLENGES AND ULTIMATE SUCCESS.

WHEN NOT IN FRONT OF THE CAMERA, ONE OF THE JOYS IN WOODARD'S LIFE IS SUPPORTING HER TWELVE-YEAR-OLD DAUGHTER'S PASSION FOR HORSES. MAVIS GOT HER FIRST HORSE AT THE AGE OF FIVE AND HAS BEEN RIDING NON-STOP EVER SINCE. THE FAMILY HAS THREE HORSES, NAMED RENOIR, SHADES OF GRAY, AND SEASHELL, BOARDED AT A BEAUTIFUL PRIVATE FACILITY JUST THIRTY MINUTES OUTSIDE OF LOS ANGELES. WOODARD BELIEVES IN HER DAUGHTER'S GIFT FOR WORKING WITH HORSES, AND IF MAVIS'S SUCCESS BOTH IN AND OUT OF THE RING IS ANY INDICATION, SHE MAY HAVE A RIDING CAREER AHEAD OF HER.

(*Authors' note*: DURING OUR INTERVIEW WITH MOTHER AND DAUGHTER THAT TOOK PLACE VIA TELEPHONE FROM MS. WOODARD'S OFFICE, MAVIS SET UP SEVERAL IRONING BOARDS AND WAS JUMPING OVER THEM IN TRUE EQUESTRIAN STYLE.)

"Watching people who love and

communicate with horses replenishes and relaxes me." For Alfre Woodard, that's especially true when her daughter, Mavis, is the one in the saddle. "Every time I watch Mavis I see this place where God is shining through, even when she is dealing with horses that are not her own. She is a horse whisperer and has been ever since she was a little girl. It gives me a very spiritual and grounded feeling watching her ride. Whether she is showing or just bathing her horse, or doing something wacky like bareback riding in her bathing suit, I am constantly amazed at her ability to communicate with horses."

"I have loved horses ever since I could talk," says Mavis. "As a little girl I would look at them and say, 'What's that, what's that?'"

Alfre agrees. "She was just over a year old and she was obsessed. When she was two, we went to visit my husband Roderick's sister who breeds horses in Massachusetts, and my little daughter rode a big stallion around the paddock. As I took her down she started to say, 'More, more.' At the age of three her father read Black Beauty to her every night. I had to call her Beauty and whinny just to get her to dress for school. I sat with her through the storm and shipwreck scene in The Black Stallion, which she watched over and over again."

"I told my mom at the age of three that I was going to start riding, but she told me that I couldn't have a horse until my fifth birthday," remembers Mavis. "So as soon as my birthday

came I said, 'Mommy, can you get me a horse?' And she did."

"Of course, when a child is three, five seems like forever, and I had hoped that she would forget about this. But of course, Mavis didn't. Our good friend's daughter, Chelsea Weaver, had outgrown a large pony named Norton that she needed to sell to advance to a higher level jumping horse. So we bought Norton and became horse owners before we intended."

Norton often had ideas of his own. "I fell off at least once a week," recalls Mavis. "One time I was riding and I really wanted to jump this bigger fence, so I jumped it. The next day I came to the exact same fence and Norton didn't want to jump it, so he stopped and I fell off and hit my head on the fence."

"When she was five she was just a little gnat, and Norton was used to a very strong rider, so he would kind of flick her off and start to bolt. He didn't really take Mavis seriously, so she went through a period where she would get nervous when it was time to go to the barn. She would say, 'I want to go but I'm nervous and I need you to help me get back on.' So we had a lot of wonderful conversations just dealing with the fear."

These mother-daughter talks proved to be a growth opportunity for Mavis. "One day when she was not feeling great about riding Norton, she told me she wanted to write a book about this experience," says Alfre. "I asked her what she wanted to say, and my six year old fired back, 'I'll call it *Facing Down Your Fear* and tell other kids that when I really concentrate on how much I love both riding and my pony, they become more important than my nervousness. If a kid got injured playing soccer, basketball, or gymnastics and they are afraid to get back to the things they really like, they could just read my book and get back to doing it.' So she went to the barn, toughed it out, and taught herself a lesson. Mavis was then able to go to the next level."

Through the years, this love of horses has helped nurture the mother-daughter relationship. "Mavis learned to ride before knowing how to add, subtract, or even write, so this love was always incorporated into what she was doing. When she was old enough that grades started to matter, I would say, 'You can ride as much as you want to, but I have to know that you are keeping up with your grades.' And she did. It is amazing to see this sense of discipline, perseverance, patience, and responsibility in such a little person. I have to respect it and, as a mother, help keep it alive."

"My mom is very involved with what I do," says Mavis.

"SAY IF YOU'VE GOT A REALLY BIG SECRET BUT YOU JUST CAN'T BEAR TO HOLD IT IN ANYMORE—YOU CAN ALWAYS TELL YOUR HORSE."

"Every Sunday on the way to the barn we have this wonderful time together. After my lessons, if I learn something new, she will write it down and talk to me about it in the car so she can understand it more. She is always there."

"When I drive out to the barn with Mavis, my cell phone isn't on. I sit there and read the paper, drink tea, and watch my daughter. It's a welcome break from the film industry for me."

Although Alfre is very clear that this is Mavis's world, she has always been drawn to and fascinated with the magic and mystery of horses. "For me, horses are a combination of power and grace coming together like no other place in creation. I have always been drawn to and fascinated with the magic and are so soulful and open that I just love being around them. I have also grown a lot watching Mavis while she is working with horses. The way she is honest with her horse is the way that I have to be as a mom. Also, as I have watched her compete in shows, it has clarified for me the sense of perseverance in my own artistic and professional life too. We have both had to work hard, demonstrate, and grow in grace with victory as well as with defeat. For Mavis, that's come from working with her horses."

"You have to be very open in the way you communicate with horses," agrees Mavis. "You can talk to them with your voice but also with your legs and your hands and the way you move. Never frighten a horse with really sudden movements; everything you do with them should be handled subtly. It is important to always be honest with your horse—you never want to fool them. You *can't* fool them. Horses are kind of like having a best friend. You can tell them things like if

you're having a rough day and it makes you feel better. Say if you've got a really big secret but you just can't bear to hold it in anymore—you can always tell your horse."

Adds Alfre, "I know that there is some danger involved with the sport, but I really believe that people are born who they are. Mavis has gotten such pure, unbridled joy from being around horses, even as a baby, that the connection is spiritual. She has a real gift for dealing with horses and I feel like this is between her and God. The ability to understand and to appreciate this particular creature—I don't fear it because it is just a pure love!"

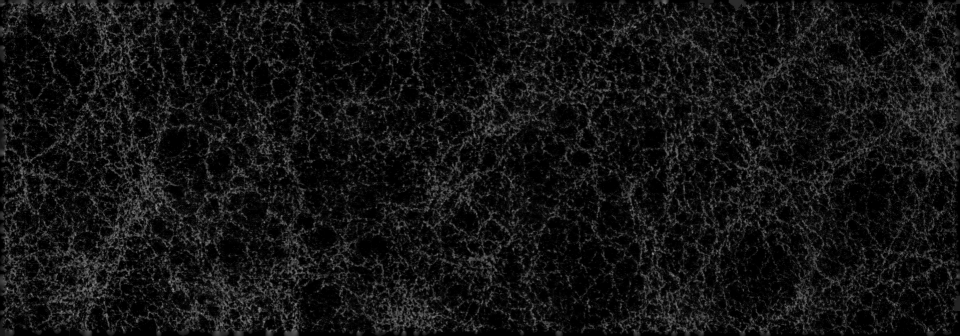

HEALING HANDS, HEALING HORSES

NEDA DEMAYO

Return to Freedom

"Close your eyes and imagine wild horses running across the open range. . . . Now close your eyes and imagine they are gone . . . forever"

In 1998, with the help of family, friends, and other concerned volunteers, Neda DeMayo founded the Return to Freedom American Wild Horse Sanctuary. Today, RTF provides refuge for more than 200 wild horses and burros—and a unique learning environment where anyone can directly experience these marvelous animals in a natural setting. The organization's programs are designed to educate through self-discovery and to nurture an appreciation for all life.

RTF is the home of Spirit, the mustang that served as the live model for the exhilarating 2002 animated film *Spirit: Stallion of the Cimarron*. "We were looking for two things," explains Ann Daly, head of the DreamWorks feature animation department, about how they came to choose RTF as the place to retire the remarkable horse, "a place that had a philosophy we were comfortable with, and a location appropriate to the personality of Spirit. We felt we found it with the American Wild Horse Sanctuary. It allowed us to make a choice that's best for Spirit's personality and to extend the message of what the movie is about."

I cannot remember a time when

I did not love horses. My mother said "horse" was one of my first spoken words, and to be near them I began riding at the age of five. I can remember seeing wild horses on television being chased by everything from cowboys to hovering helicopters and wanting to help them escape and have a place for them to re-

main free, together, and safe. As I grew up, my relationship with horses deepened and I began to think about somehow, some way to start a sanctuary for wild horses. Years later, living on the West Coast, I read about the wild horse adoptions sponsored by the Bureau of Land Management and how some of the horses, because they could not be domesticated, were being slaughtered. Despite the best of intentions, the programs were failing. I felt compelled to do something about it.

So in 1997 I took action to make my dream a reality. With the help of my family, I purchased a rundown three-hundred-acre ranch in the hills above Santa Barbara and created a refuge for wild horses. We have been able to relocate entire herds to RTF, where they are thriving because they are together in their natural family and social groups. We have also been working with various experts on natural and non-intrusive population management programs so we don't have to separate the stallions from their herds. Return to Freedom has garnered support and interest as a model program because of our innovative approach to natural herd management. RTF is unique in this aspect and has chosen this approach as an alternative to separating mares from stallions and disrupting natural social groups, behavior, and evolution. We have and continue to inspire change in wild horse and sanctuary management.

RTF functions as a living-history museum so that people can see the important role the horse has played in the development of our country, our cultural history, as well as their importance as an integral part of the ecosystem. At the sanctuary, people can be introduced to the American Wild Horse of today, which includes a diversity of origins. After genera-

> # "AS STEWARDS OF THIS WORLD, I BELIEVE WE HAVE A RESPONSIBILITY TO MAINTAIN A HEALTHY BALANCE BETWEEN OUR DESIRES AND THE NEEDS OF OTHER CREATURES AND THE ENVIRONMENT."

tions of surviving on their own, in harsh environments, they have earned their status as a wild horse.

American Wild Horses have evolved over five hundred years from Spanish bloodlines, Cavalry remount horses after World War I, and draft horse stock, for the most part. All the horses at the sanctuary are ambassadors, representative of our living history and their unique origins. In addition to our rescue and sanctuary efforts, RTF has a preservation program that includes isolated genetic groups of horses, many with documented historical significance.

Our Sulphur Springs herd, with their color and unique striping, as well as their DNA, connects them with the primitive Iberian Sorraia, dating back to 25,000 B.C. The Cerbats, the Kigers, the Wilbur-Cruce Colonial Mission horses, the Bashkir Curlies, and the various open-range horses all help us celebrate the diversity of wild horses in America.

Horses are a symbol of freedom and the American spirit, just like the bald eagle. In the animated movie *Spirit*, both animals travel across the plains side-by-side. That's why it was particularly thrilling that RTF was chosen by DreamWorks SKG, the company that produced the movie, to be the home of the horse that the movie's drawings, animation, and spirit were based on.

Human beings have a tendency to see the natural world as a threat, as something they need to conquer, enhance, or profit from. In the process, we often destroy the things we love and the things we need. As stewards of this world, I believe we have a responsibility to maintain a healthy balance between our desires and the needs of other creatures and the environment. For example, I enjoy riding horses, and I benefit from my relationship with all kinds of horses. I feel strongly that wild horses have intricate social structures and communities. Their culture is in danger of being lost forever as they continue to be eradicated from their homelands. I am extremely proud of Return to Freedom's role in providing inspiration to better understand and appreciate their freedom.

RTF, by it's very nature, is an educational environment where children and adults come to learn directly from nature and animals. To preserve and protect habitat and wildlife species while engaging the human is not only powerful but necessary for the future health of the Earth and it's inhabitants.

Creating a value and respect for things as they are, because they are, is, in my opinion, the only hope for a new human being to emerge.

HILARY DUFF

Making a Difference

HILARY DUFF HAS BECOME INDELIBLY ETCHED INTO THE HEARTS AND MINDS OF "TWEENS" AROUND THE WORLD ON THE STRENGTH OF HER WINNING AND SLIGHTLY QUIRKY AND KLUTZY PERFORMANCE ON THE MEGA-HIT TELEVISION SHOW, *Lizzie McGuire*. THE SIXTEEN-YEAR-OLD PHENOM HAS ALREADY STARRED IN FOUR MUCH-TALKED-ABOUT FILMS, INCLUDING *Agent Cody Banks*, *The Lizzie McGuire Movie*, *Cheaper by the Dozen*, AND, IN 2004, *A Cinderella Story*.

ON THE HEELS OF HER BIG-SCREEN SUCCESS, HILARY HAS BRANCHED OUT INTO MUSIC, RECORDING A CHRISTMAS ALBUM IN 2002, PERFORMING ON THE PLATINUM-SELLING *Lizzie McGuire Movie* SOUNDTRACK, AND IN THE FALL OF 2003 RELEASING HER OWN CD, *Metamorphosis*, THAT HIT NUMBER ONE ON THE MUSIC CHARTS. HILARY HAS ALSO RECENTLY LAUNCHED HER OWN FASHION LINE, APTLY NAMED STUFF BY HILARY DUFF, WHICH IS BEING SOLD EXCLUSIVELY AT TARGET STORES ACROSS THE COUNTRY.

GROWING UP ON A FAMILY RANCH OUTSIDE OF AUSTIN, TEXAS, HILARY HAS ALWAYS HAD A PASSION FOR HORSES. DEEPLY PHILANTHROPIC, SHE HAS COMBINED HER LOVE OF THESE ANIMALS WITH AN IMPORTANT CAUSE, SERVING AS YOUTH AMBASSADOR FOR RETURN TO FREEDOM, THE AMERICAN WILD HORSE SANCTUARY, LOCATED JUST THIRTY MILES NORTH OF SANTA BARBARA, WHERE SHE WAS PHOTOGRAPHED FOR THE BOOK. HER INVOLVEMENT WITH RTF WILL INCLUDE SPEARHEADING THE SPONSOR-A-HORSE NATIONAL CLASSROOM PROGRAM THAT WILL HELP RAISE MUCH-NEEDED FUNDS FOR TAKING CARE OF THE MORE THAN TWO HUNDRED WILD HORSES CURRENTLY AT THE SANCTUARY.

I've loved riding and being around horses

ever since I was little. My family owns a ranch outside of Austin with lots of land and a great house, and my parents used to put my older sister, Haylie, and me on the ponies when we were babies. We may have been just about able to sit up, but we knew we had to hold on tight.

I started riding at the age of four, and for the next several years Haylie and I were lucky enough to have two Shetland ponies and a Welsh. Our favorites were the brown and white brother and sister Shetlands that we named Cinnamon and Sugar. They were really beautiful and quite small—the perfect size for us. Cinnamon was mine. She had a bit of a diva attitude with others, but she was really very sweet with me.

Lady was a beautiful older Welsh pony that we had, too, but unfortunately she died when she ate too much clover and foundered. A few years ago, Haylie and I were going through

our photo albums of us with the ponies and we recalled how gentle Lady really was with us. Right then and there, both of us realized how lucky we were to grow up with horses.

I think having a special animal in your life can help anyone learn to appreciate nature more. And a horse can become your best friend, just like a dog. Both have a strong sense of loyalty. Of course, it's hard for some people to have horses because they may not have enough space to keep them. When I was eight or nine, we moved to Los Angeles and we could no longer have horses, so we gave the ponies to some family friends. But I still ride, and two years ago I started taking lessons again at the Equestrian Center in Burbank. With everything happening for me now, my schedule is so busy, but I do find time to go with my friends to the Equestrian Center for a trail ride sometimes. There's nothing I love more than getting out of the city environment and having some fun.

I feel so fortunate to be in a position where young people maybe see me as a role model. It's important for kids to know that they can make a positive difference. It's very cool that they see me on TV and say, "Oh, she's really cool and I want to be like her." My sister is my role model. I also look up to people

who are involved with organizations that are helping people or animals. When I first heard how the group Return to Freedom is protecting wild mustangs that no longer have land to roam around free, I knew that I wanted to get involved with this cause. It is so great that the mustangs have this land where they can still be wild. If their land and freedom were taken away for good, these wild horses would be in real danger of becoming extinct—and we must not let that happen. I'm helping Return to Freedom get more land so that they can rescue and bring more horses to the sanctuary.

Another charity that I work with is Kids with a Cause. It's a grassroots organization that matches celebrity children with youngsters who are poor, in foster care, or sick. It would be so great to bring some of them to Return to Freedom. Horses, especially the wild ones, are so mysterious and intriguing that you feel invincible and get such a rush when you are riding them. I'd like these kids to feel that.

As for me, when I am older I want to have my own ranch with horses. And when I have children I definitely want horses to be a part of their lives, just as they've been an important part of mine.

"As for me, when I am older I want to have my own ranch with horses. And when I have children I definitely want horses to be a part of their lives, just as they've been an important part of mine."

ANDREA EASTMAN

The Premarin Foals

ANDREA EASTMAN IS ONE OF THE MOST SUCCESSFUL THEATRICAL AGENTS IN THE ENTERTAINMENT BUSINESS. AS A SENIOR VICE PRESIDENT AT INTERNATIONAL CREATIVE MANAGEMENT, ONE OF THE WORLD'S LARGEST TALENT AGENCIES, EASTMAN OVERSEES THE CAREER OF SUCH STARS AS RICHARD GERE, SYLVESTER STALLONE, AND STOCKARD CHANNING. SHE WAS A CASTING DIRECTOR FOR *The Godfather* AND *Love Story* AND WAS RESPONSIBLE FOR PUTTING ALI MACGRAW IN HER FIRST FILM. THE TWO WOMEN ARE STILL BEST FRIENDS, AND BOTH ARE MAJOR ANIMAL ACTIVISTS.

HAVING A LIFELONG LOVE OF HORSES AND OTHER ANIMALS, EASTMAN BECAME OUTRAGED WHEN SHE LEARNED THAT THE HORMONE REPLACEMENT DRUG PREMARIN WAS MADE FROM THE URINE OF PREGNANT MARES, AND THAT MOST OF THEIR NEWBORN FOALS WENT TO SLAUGHTER. TAKING ACTION, SHE BECAME INVOLVED WITH UNITED PEGASUS SIX YEARS AGO, A NONPROFIT ORGANIZATION THAT RESCUES RETIRED RACEHORSES AND PREMARIN MARES AND FOALS.

I will never forget for as long as I live

the night that I saved my Lucky. It was a stormy October evening when this teeny Appaloosa, about the size of a golden retriever, was led out of this huge van. He almost fell over backwards and he was gasping for breath because he was so terrified. I stayed at the barn until midnight, feeding him hay and stroking him until he started to calm down. When I finally left him and was walking back to the house, the clouds parted, and shining in the sky above me was the brightest star I had ever seen. Right then and there I named my little foal Lucky Star. He will be with me forever.

Lucky is a Premarin foal. These are horses that are born to mares that have been impregnated for their urine, which is used to make the hormone-replacement drug Premarin. The pregnant mares are attached to a machine that milks them for their urine; most are stall-bound for eleven months. Sometimes water is withheld from the poor mares so that their urine gets more concentrated.

When the foals are born they are taken away from their mothers any time from between one to five months, and the mares are impregnated again almost immediately after the birth of their babies. It is heart wrenching to hear mothers and babies cry for each other as they are separated and to watch these foals suckle each other because they do not have mothers. The foals are then sent to auction and slaughtered for their meat, which is sold to countries abroad where young horsemeat is a delicacy.

For the last six years, my mission in life has been to help save Premarin foals. I have probably helped to rescue almost a thousand of these babies from this barbaric practice by raising money for United Pegasus. At auction the foals are purchased in groups of twenty or thirty, and rescue buyers will bid against the slaughter buyers. Most of the rescued babies are sent to the United Pegasus Sanctuary or to people across the country who have adopted them. Lucky is one of two Premarin foals that I personally own. They both have grown up to be such wonderful horses.

I rescued Shawnee, a beautiful Paint, when he was two months old and was so little that he almost died. Like Lucky, he was delivered in a big truck with twenty other loose foals; somehow, the handler got him out of there without being trampled. Since then, Shawnee has grown into a magnificent animal, and he absolutely loves my husband. It's touching to see him put his head on Richard's chest.

My work is just a drop in the bucket when you realize how many of these foals need to be rescued. In the past, as many as seventy thousand foals have been killed in just one year. That number is down now, but not enough. My goal is to have every person in this country know what a Premarin foal is so that, someday, there will be no more.

"IT IS HEART WRENCHING TO HEAR MOTHERS AND BABIES CRY FOR EACH OTHER AS THEY ARE SEPARATED."

RUSSELL MEANS

The Lakota Way

Described as the most famous American Indian since Sitting Bull and Crazy Horse, Oglala/Lakota Sioux Russell Means made a name for himself as an activist two decades before he became an actor. In 1970 he became the first national director of AIM, the American Indian Movement, and was very involved with the government standoff at the now infamous Wounded Knee. As a political activist, Means ran for President as the Libertarian candidate in 1988, wanting to voice his opposition to both the Democrat and Republican frontrunners.

The 1990s launched a whole new career for Means as an actor and performer. He starred in the memorable role of Chingachgook in *The Last of the Mohicans*, as The Chief in *Wagons East!*, and as Old Indian in *Natural Born Killers*, and he was the voice of Chief Powhatan in Disney's animated feature *Pocahontas*. He is also an accomplished artist and author of his national best-selling autobiography, *Where White Men Fear to Tread*.

Committed to keeping the Lakota Sioux history and knowledge alive, Means and his family donated 160 acres in Porcupine, South Dakota, on the Pine Ridge Sioux Reservation for the establishment of a Treaty, or Total

Immersion School, designed by the Maori Peoples in New Zealand. This unique program, a private school for kindergarten through third grade, focuses on the culture of the indigenous population. This is the first Total Immersion School for American Indians in the United States. Means has also started a horse breeding program in Porcupine to help reintroduce the traditions of the Lakota horse culture to the children so that the Lakota way of life will not be lost.

The Lakota Total Immersion School

that we have just started in South Dakota means exactly that—total immersion in the early Lakota Sioux way of life. We are not going to teach the three R's of reading, writing, and arithmetic. Like primitive peoples around the world, our society has a strong oral tradition, and so our culture stresses the three L's: listen, look, and learn. In a society that has this verbal emphasis, listening is the first step toward giving respect. The Lakota believe that we have to listen to the world in order to understand and live in harmony with those that inhabit the universe.

At the school we are teaching the Lakota way in working with and riding horses, through friendship and not intimidation. If this relationship starts at a very young age, it benefits the entire community and that individual's life forever. So we have started a preschool program that will begin a child's lifelong association and friendship with a horse. This has been what is missing from our now patriarchal society, the ability for men to nurture, as it is not inherent in their nature. If you are introduced to this kind of life at a very young age, though, it becomes natural. What our male students learn through horsemanship helps them mature into manhood. The school, however, is for boys and girls, and both the parents and children become very involved in what is going on here.

There are nine horses at the school right now, and the children are learning how to listen to and respect them. They will have the opportunity to care for and ride the horses as well as learn about their history and culture as they get older. During the last thirty years, most Lakota children have not had this opportunity. Of course, it has to be a nurturing relationship and not a cruel one, like the way so many South

Dakota cowboys used to treat their horses. I watched them once when I was twelve years old tie up the horses' feet and then get on their back so that they couldn't buck. This type of "breaking" will totally break the horse's spirit.

As a Lakota Sioux, I come from a very strong matriarchal society, as do most of the Indians of the Western Hemisphere. The Plains Indians, which includes the Lakota and many other tribes, believe that the horse is a male animal and that the dog is a female animal. With the male, the horse is a friend but he always tries to take advantage of the women. Originally there were four different strains of horses that were used and ridden by the Lakota. They were black, sorrel, Palomino, and white. Although we tried to keep the stallions with their respective herds of mares so they would not be aggressive, natural selection frequently happened, so that the horses ultimately ended up traveling the plains with whatever group they chose.

Coming from a horse culture, I remember my first interactions with horses. I grew up on the Yankton Sioux Indian Reservation in South Dakota where my grandparents and great-grandma raised horses, not just for pleasure but also for work. At the age of four I was helping my grandpa harness the team. Being so small, I wasn't really strong enough to work the horses, but nevertheless he let me hold the reins of the team. They would get away from me once in a while and go into the cornfield and start eating the corn. But grandpa never reprimanded me or took away the reins. He let me struggle with them and then when I wasn't strong enough to get those horses out of the field, he would ask me if he could take over. And I sure was happy then!

I also remember that when I was eleven years old, my

"The Lakota believe that we have to listen to the world in order to understand and live in harmony with those that inhabit the universe."

153

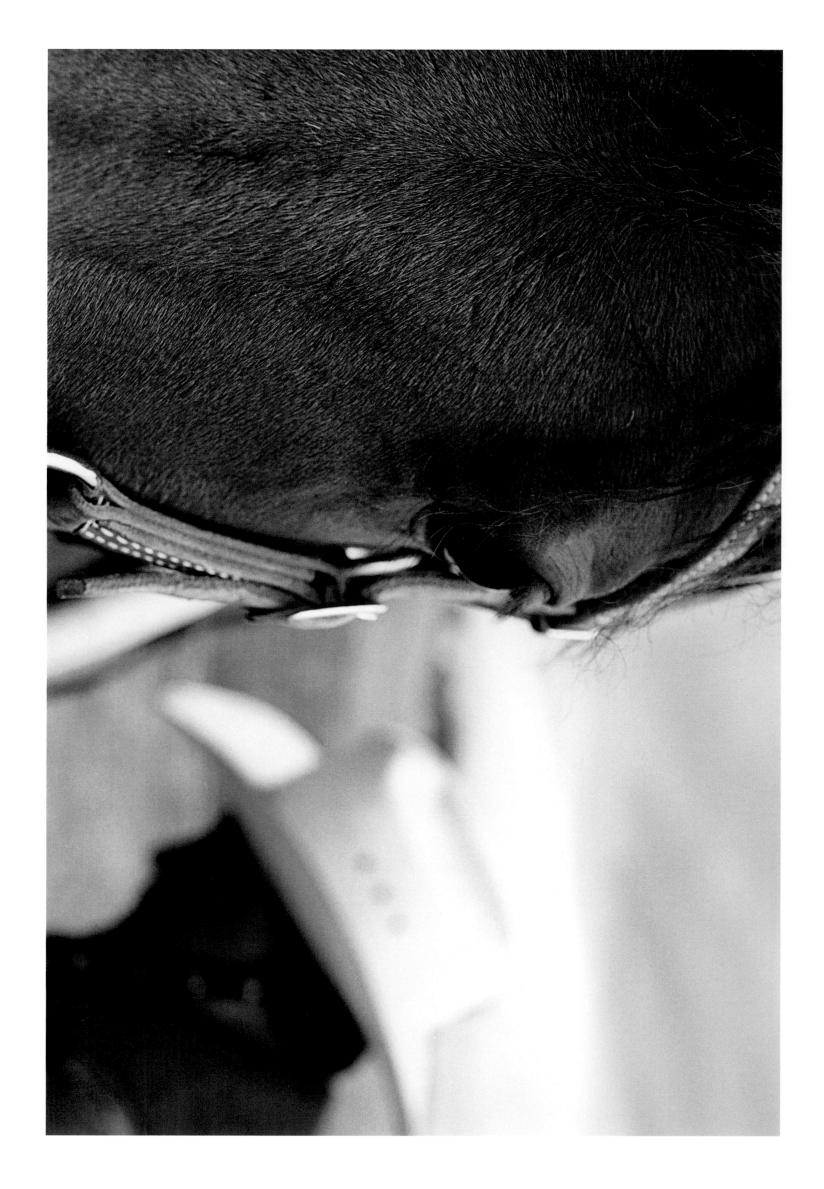

auntie Madonna had a horse named Pal, and everyone considered him to be an old plug. I had to go get him out of the pasture every morning because Madonna couldn't catch him.

My grandpa never made me feel like I was a failure, especially around horses, and this is the environment we are creating at the school. My family would always tell me that you treat animals, birds, and even insects better than you treat human beings. If you show them respect, they will respect you back. This is also true for our grandmother, the Earth. You show her respect and thankfulness and she will continue to provide the bounty that is necessary for us all to live on this Earth.

When you raise a horse the Indian way, it takes seven, eight, nine years to completely train him. We believe that it takes at least that long to familiarize yourself and get into sync with a horse. But you don't select your horse after it is born. It is your duty to develop a relationship with the mare before she gives birth, and when the foal is born it will be your horse. You treat the both the mare and unborn foal with the utmost of consideration by talking to them, giving her the best of food, and playing music around them.

When my horse Trigger was born, I tore the birthing sack off of him myself so that the first thing he smelled was me, even before his mother. Trigger and I bonded and he became my horse instantly. A horse that is worked properly for seven or eight years will always protect you. I grew up with horses that

as soon as you fell off would stop and wait for you to remount.

Growing up, we couldn't afford saddles, so we always rode bareback, which allows you to get to know the horse even better. You can feel the horse's muscles, and this creates even better communication between you and the horse. Indians know that animals are always trying to communicate with human beings, and it is our responsibility to listen. Once you develop the ability to listen, you then learn how to communi-

> "ONCE YOU DEVELOP THE ABILITY TO LISTEN, YOU THEN LEARN HOW TO COMMUNICATE."

cate. This happens with horse people all over the world, although not with all of them. I was taking a tour of a Lipizzaner farm in southeastern Wisconsin, and the owner made a statement that was totally contrary to what horses are all about. He said, "It is very costly to train these horses, and by the time we get to the stupid ones who refuse to get trained, we have already put six years into them." I didn't say anything, but I thought to myself

that they are the smart ones! Also, historically Indians never put a bit in a horse's mouth, although things are changing because we have had so much non-Indian interference.

These are the kinds of awarenesses and relationships that we are teaching at the TREATY school. What children and families learn will help to bring back the matriarchal way of life into our society. The Lakota has only vestiges of this culture left. With each generation we get further and further away from it. This school is the beginning of the reversal of that colonial process.

CLEA NEWMAN

Pegasus Therapeutic Riding

It makes a lot of sense that Clea Newman would make helping others her life's work. After all, she is the daughter of renowned actors and philanthropists Paul Newman and Joanne Woodward. In addition to Newman's Own Inc., a food company that has raised more than $150 million for thousands of charities since its inception in 1982, and the Hole in the Wall Gang Camp, which directly benefits seriously ill children who attend the camp yearly free of charge, the family is also involved in the Pegasus Therapeutic Riding program, where Clea combines her passion for horses with her desire to live her life with meaning. Clea is the organization's director of development, while Joanne is a member of the honorary board of directors, and Paul often lends his talents at events for the nonprofit organization.

Pegasus began in 1975 with the help of a few volunteers who believed in the therapeutic power of horseback riding. Starting with eight physically disabled students, Pegasus today serves more than 240 people, aged four to seventy-four, at eight locations in New York and Connecticut. Highly qualified instructors and therapists oversee the dedicated core of 250 volunteers, who help students achieve their therapy goals while reaching for the stars. The program is seen as so successful that there is a waiting list of more than 300 children and adults.

As important as the staff and volunteers are to Pegasus Therapeutic Riding, the heart and soul of the organization are the well-trained horses that seem to sense how important their jobs are and the special needs of their charges. As Clea so aptly says, "These horses and ponies are as close to angels as you can get here on earth."

I was actually working for my dad's camp,

The Hole in the Wall Gang, when Pegasus approached me. Although I wasn't looking for another job at the time, when I realized it was the Therapeutic Riding program my sister had volunteered for and spoke so highly of, I came in for the interview and took the job immediately. It couldn't have been a better fit for me. Working with horses to therapeutically help disabled people—it just doesn't get better than that! It wasn't until I started to work there and wrote my first letter that I noticed that the stationery listed my mother's name as an honorary board member, and I said, "Geez, you guys are everywhere!"

Pegasus works with people of all different ages and disabilities, from the visually impaired to those with cerebral palsy, Down syndrome, Attention Deficit Disorder, even stroke victims and amputees. It is not uncommon for children with ADD to utter the horse command "Walk on!" as their first words. The rhythmic motion of the horses also slows down children with autism and allows them to sort out their thoughts and to think more clearly.

In the eleven years that I have been with Pegasus, there have been some absolutely remarkable almost-miracles. There was one child who had cerebral palsy and was completely nonverbal. When he first got on a horse, all the muscles in his body were contorted and he couldn't stretch out his legs. After attending the program regularly for a few years, he was able to relax his leg muscles and walk better. One day his mom and I started watching him ride when he suddenly turned and looked at her and said, "Hi, Mom!" She and I just looked at each other and our jaws dropped. It the first word he had ever spoken. His mother burst into tears.

Another remarkable story involves a five-year-old boy who was very bright, but because he couldn't see, always looked down and was very, very shy. After several years of riding he has come out of his shell and even has his own talk show on the local radio station. Riding helps visually impaired people with their sense of balance and centering their bodies in space. On a horse they can feel the wind in their face and an incredible sense of movement as they are trotted around.

> ## "THE CHANGE IN THESE KIDS' PERSONALITIES AND THEIR ABILITY TO FUNCTION BETTER, ALONG WITH THEIR INCREASED SELF-CONFIDENCE, IS JUST EXTRAORDINARY."
>
> —PAUL NEWMAN

It's amazing to see how the horses we work with completely understand their job and take it seriously. We had one high-spirited pony named Bart that would practically get down on his knees to get close to the kids. I have discovered that horses are so trusting, if you don't break that trust, they will give you their heart and soul.

My parents are great supporters of Pegasus, and that really means a lot to me. My mom says, "Even for kids who have a mental rather than physical disability, having the brain do two things at once when they work with both their hands and legs focuses the mind and helps them to coordinate. It's astounding."

Each spring, Pegasus has a horse show for the riders, and we have the chance to award the children their ribbons. My mom says, "It is among the best opportunities in our lives," and my dad adds that "The change in these kids' personalities and their ability to function better, along with their increased self-confidence, is just extraordinary. It all comes from the ability to handle a twelve-hundred-pound horse."

Horses have always been an important part of my life, and

"HORSES ARE SO TRUSTING, IF YOU DON'T BREAK THAT TRUST, THEY WILL GIVE YOU THEIR HEART AND SOUL."

for the longest time I thought I would become a professional rider. I took it very seriously and performed well in amateur competitions. That's all I did as a young girl—went to school and rode horses. But I realized that to advance I would have to show eleven months out of the year and I didn't want to live on the road all the time. I still own three horses, but two are retired, so Katrinka, my lovely Dutch warmblood, is the only horse that I show now. She has a perfect big white heart on her forehead with a little brown spot in the middle. She also makes me laugh. She is very expressive in every thing she does, very flamboyant. After making a beautiful jump she will buck or make this funny face at me. I spend more time riding around the ring laughing than I do being serious because we have so much fun together.

Both my parents have ridden, but my mom was somewhat afraid of horses at first. One day when I was twelve or thirteen and showing in Santa Barbara, I came out of the ring after not having a very good round and she looked at me and said, "Oh, honey, you were wonderful!" Well, I wasn't wonderful! "I was horrible, mom." She, of course,

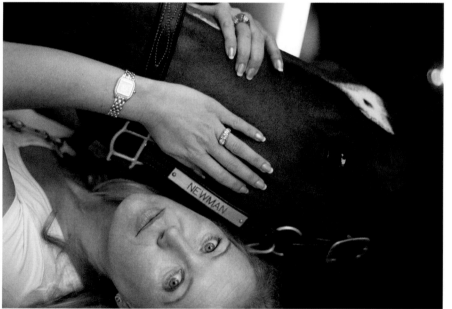

said, "Sweetie, I thought you were perfect." Right then and there I told her that she should try riding. So I had her ride my wonderful older grayish dapple horse named Nothin' Doin' (Doey) with a big old head and huge ears. Doey loved my mother and would docilely trot around the ring with her. One time she was doing a little combination of two or three jumps, and he made a nice big jump over the final one and my mom lost her balance and got wrapped up around his neck. Her whole upper body was in front of the saddle, and that horse carried her around the ring so that she wouldn't fall off. Finally I yelled, "Mom, just say whoa!" When she did, Doey walked up to the end of the ring and put his head over the fence with a sigh of relief, and mom climbed back into her saddle. My dad was really impressed because she overcame her fear and even showed with me at Santa Barbara a few years later.

The last eleven years have been wonderful. It's a great feeling to work at a place where our prime objective is to help others. As my mother used to say, "If you are really feeling sad, the best thing is to go and do something for someone else."

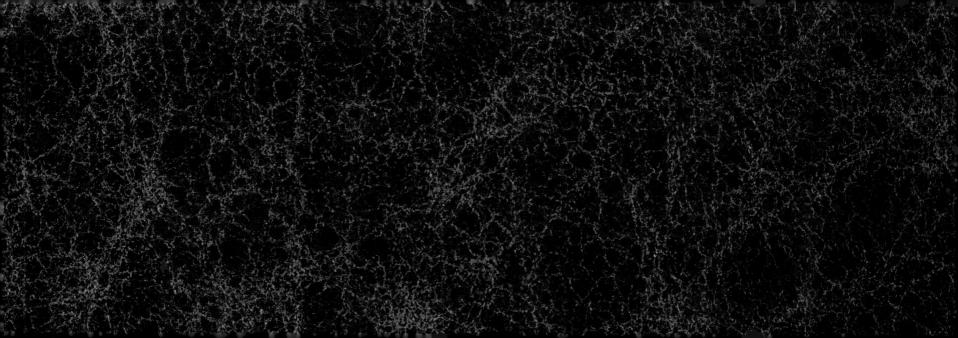

ABOUT THE AUTHORS

JILL RAPPAPORT

My Horses Are Not Imaginary Anymore

MILLIONS OF VIEWERS HAVE COME TO KNOW JILL RAPPAPORT AS THE ENTERTAINMENT CORRESPONDENT FOR THE COUNTRY'S NUMBER ONE FAVORITE MORNING SHOW, NBC'S *Today*. SHE BEGAN HER CAREER AS A PUBLICIST FOR UNITED ARTISTS, WORKING WITH CELEBRITIES AND DIRECTORS ON SUCH FILMS AS *Rocky, Manhattan,* AND *Apocalypse Now,* AND SHE MADE HER ON-AIR DEBUT AT THE NBC AFFILIATE IN SAN FRANCISCO. BUT THE BAY AREA COULDN'T HOLD ONTO HER FOR LONG. RAPPAPORT WAS SELECTED TO HOST NEW YORK'S COVETED PRIME-TIME SHOW *PM Magazine* WITH MATT LAUER. FROM THERE SHE WENT TO WCBS-TV IN NEW YORK, WHERE SHE BE-CAME THE STATION'S POPULAR ENTER-TAINMENT CORRESPONDENT FOR THE

NEXT FIVE YEARS. IN ADDITION, SHE HOSTED THE WELL-KNOWN MOVIE SHOW *Flix* FOR VH1.

IN 1991, NBC'S *Today* CAME KNOCKING ON HER DOOR, AND RAPPAPORT, A NATIVE OF BLOOMFIELD HILLS, MICHIGAN, WAS NAMED THE SHOW'S EXCLUSIVE ENTERTAINMENT CORRESPONDENT. DURING HER CAREER SHE LANDED INTERVIEWS WITH ENTERTAIN-MENT LEGENDS INCLUDING AUDREY HEPBURN, LUCILLE BALL, JAMES STEWART, ELIZABETH TAYLOR, AND BARBRA STREISAND.

WHEN RAPPAPORT'S NOT WORKING THE RED CARPET, YOU CAN FIND HER RIDING HER BELOVED HORSES, SUNDANCE AND OREO, WITH HER FOUR DOGS TRAILING ALONG AT HER LAST BUCK RANCH IN WATERMILL, NEW YORK.

I first realized I was obsessed with horses

when I was four years old. I was in the car with my parents, and all of a sudden a horse trailer pulled up alongside us. All I could see from the backseat was a tush and tail. Well, I was beside myself, and the love affair began. As I got a little older, I would walk down the street to a house that had a white four-rail fence that resembled those beautiful Thoroughbred farms in Kentucky, and I would sit on that fence and pretend it was my ranch. Then I proceeded to put my hand in the air, as if I were petting a real horse—my horse. I had quite the imagination, and the neighbors must have thought I was nuts, considering how ridiculous I looked.

No one else in my family was into riding, except when we would take our annual spring vacations to Tucson, Arizona, and we would stay at these great dude ranches, the Eldorado and the Tanque Verde Ranch, which is still there. Ironically, my sister Linda, an incredible photographer, was a better rider than I was; the wranglers told her she had a "great seat." She was hoping that meant she looked good in her jeans . . . Linda definitely could not understand where I got this crazy passion from, a passion that my father later said gave him every gray hair on his head.

I started taking riding lessons at the age of seven and had a few spills and tumbles. I broke both wrists—falling off a pony, would you believe. But that did not stop me from getting back in the saddle again. My lessons continued every Sunday for the next five years at Outland Stables in Bloomfield Hills, Michigan. A day did not go by that I did not drive my parents crazy to buy me a horse. I was relentless. Finally, my mother and father gave in when my school counselor,

named Mr. Gilster (God bless him), said to them, "You would be making a terrible mistake by not getting your daughter a horse—she loves them so much, and you should never deny your child her passion."

Well, I got my wish—a beautiful bay sixteen-hand Quarter Horse mare named Missy, short for Miss Handy King, right off the famed King Ranch in Texas. She was perfect. And the people who sold her to us were so lovely, which tells you a lot. Half the battle of finding a great horse is finding a seller you can trust. They loved Missy so much that we had to meet their approval before they would sell her to us. Well, I passed the test, and I had that wonderful animal until I was seventeen years old. Then I became more interested in boys than in horses. I was also getting ready to go to college out of state, so keeping her was almost impossible.

Let me tell you, it was the saddest day of my life when we did sell her. Even my dad cried that day, not only because he had grown so fond of Missy, but also because this represented a new chapter in my life. He had watched me grow up on her. I will never forget my very first horse show, where I won my first blue ribbon. Just as I was taking a very proud bow, my dad walks up, smiling ear to ear, and puts one arm around me, the other one on my horse, and boasts, "That's my girl, and that's our horse," as if she were Hoss Cartwright. I cracked up. Little did anyone know how terrified he was of horses, and how he and my mother tried desperately to encourage me to find another safer sport. "How about tennis?" they would say, "You don't have to feed the racket."

Well, even though those teenage boys have come and gone, my passion for horses remains embedded in my soul,

and I was finally able to realize my dream of having them in my own backyard. I have a wonderful log cabin in the Hamptons that I bought in 1995, complete with pastures and a beautiful red barn—my own Ponderosa in the middle of Long Island. Here I have my Palomino horse, Sundance, and my black-and-white Paint, Oreo. I am living my childhood dream. My Last Buck Ranch—I chose that name because my last bucks are all invested here—is the most special and unique property. When you drive down the long road surrounded by sixty-foot pine trees you really feel like you're in Utah or Montana. I am able to ride my horses right up to my door. In fact, they are so spoiled that they have tried to come into the house. Hey, if the beds could support them, they would be living here. The property is surrounded by fifty acres of protected land, with wonderful trails throughout, and I am ten minutes from the ocean. One of these days I am hoping to take them to the beach and go galloping along the shore.

When I pull into the driveway, Sundance and Oreo whinny at me, and I truly feel that I am home. Life here is 180 degrees from my job on the *Today Show*, but I absolutely have the best of both worlds. When I interviewed Elizabeth Taylor for the first time, I told her how much I loved *National Velvet* and that the movie was one of the reasons I became so obsessed with horses. We both laughed about it because she felt the same way. That film changed her life and career as well.

It is so wonderful to be able to look out of your window at your own horses grazing. I love to go into their stalls and give Sundance and Oreo carrots and kisses, and I can spend hours just watching them run and play. Now I go out, sit on my own fence, and pet them for real. I no longer have to be content with my imaginary horse.

LINDA SOLOMON

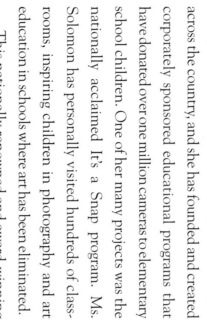

As a photojournalist, Linda Solomon reveals the heart of her subjects; through her actions, she has shared her own heart. She has divided her career between capturing the most famous personalities of our time and teaching others to express themselves through photography. "I have always believed you have to help and encourage others," said Ms. Solomon, who was honored nationally with a Distinguished Women's Award from Northwood University. She teaches her photographic techniques across the country, and she has founded and created corporately sponsored educational programs that have donated over one million cameras to elementary school children. One of her many projects was the nationally acclaimed It's a Snap program. Ms. Solomon has personally visited hundreds of classrooms, inspiring children in photography and art education in schools where art has been eliminated.

This nationally renowned and award-winning photojournalist has produced unique photo essays as a television correspondent for ABC TV's Good Morning America, and her photo essays have also been featured on World News Tonight, CNN, CBS's The Early Show, and the Lifetime Network.

Known for her use of natural light, Ms. Solomon has been commissioned by numerous celebrities. Her work is included in the collections of Ms. Elizabeth Taylor, Mr. Tony Bennett, and the late Al Hirschfeld. Her work has also been featured in numerous books, and her author's portraits have appeared on books by Elmore Leonard, Robert James Waller, author of The Bridges of Madison County, and others.

In addition to gallery exhibitions, Linda has the distinction of having the first one-woman show in the history of the famed New York Friars Club. Her photos of the Academy Awards have been featured in one-woman exhibitions across the country and featured in photo retrospectives on Good Morning America, CNN, and CBS.

A former Detroit News columnist and entertainment correspondent for CBS in Detroit, she has been selected Artist of the Year in Michigan. Linda lives with her husband, Barry, and their pooch, Chance, and kitty, Ozzie, in Bloomfield Hills, Michigan, and Tucson, Arizona.

"It has always been just me, a camera, and natural light. A camera teaches you to not just look but really see life and express your heart. I try to reveal heart in a portrait, and place my subject in light that captures heart.

"Everything started when I was five years old and my parents gave me my first camera. I also remember opening a beautifully wrapped gift to find a blue leather book with the following words engraved in gold: HAPPY 13TH BIRTHDAY, I LOVE YOU, DAD. It was a very sophisticated and elegant photo album. This treasured gift symbolized my dad's encouragement and respect for his daughter's love of photography. That's something that I have carried with me throughout my life—a life-changing gift of love, just as Jill's first horse changed her life. I learned by watching her at the stable how a horse teaches a teenager responsibility and the love of a true friend, a lifelong love."

WENDY WILKINSON

Wendy Wilkinson is the co-author of the critically acclaimed *Parents at Last: Celebrating Adoption and the New Pathways to Parenthood.* Comprised of personal stories and intimate photographs of parents around the country and such notables as U.S. Senator John McCain, LeVar and Stephanie Burton, and cartoonist Cathy Guisewite, *Parents at Last* chronicles the changing face of the contemporary American family. As an expert and author, Wendy has appeared in such publications as the *Rocky Mountain News* and *New Jersey Star Ledger,* and on many national and regional television shows across the country including CNN, *Donny & Marie, E! News Daily,* and ABC in Denver.

A freelance writer for more than a decade with a Master's degree in Journalism, her work has been published in many national and regional publications. Her first-person narrative on the Rolling Stones landed on page one of the *Los Angeles Times* "Life and Style" section, and she currently writes lifestyle and health pieces for *Fit* magazine and cover stories for Colorado-based *SpringsStyle* magazine.

In addition, Wendy has been a public relations executive for more than 20 years and currently specializes in the equine and western worlds. A horse owner since the age of ten, she now lives in Manitou Springs, Colorado, with her husband and young daughter and boards her beloved bronze Quarter Horse Chief at the Academy Riding Stables. Having access to more than 44,000 acres of Rocky Mountain trails, her perfect ride is in the spring when "the trails and surrounding hillsides are awash in scarlet indian paintbrush and bright purple lupine or the fall when the aspen glow changes from yellow to gold.

"As I approach the spacious stable grounds I turn off my cell phone, buckle on my spurs, adjust my favorite old hat, and saddle up an always-welcoming Chief. We trot off onto an isolated tree canopied trail with the Rocky Mountains looming ahead as my anchor. Breaking into an easy lope, I realize what a perfect union this horse and rider have achieved."

169

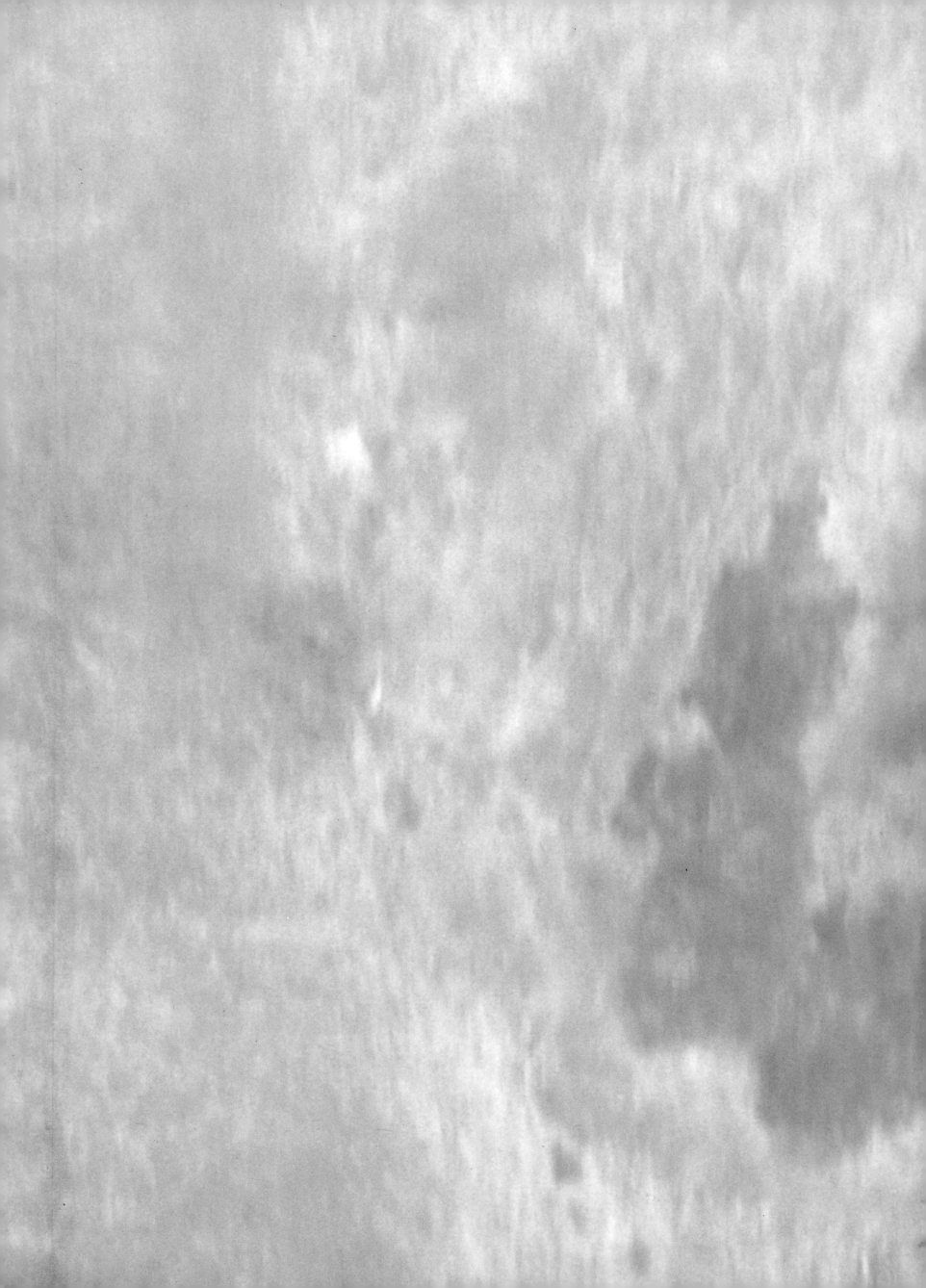